LOOKING BACK AT BRITAIN

THATCHER'S BRITAIN

1980s

THATCHER'S BRITAIN

1980s

James Harpur

 Reader's Digest | gettyimages

DAILY STAR JOIN OUR FIGHT FOR THE PENSIONERS

ANOTHER DAILY STAR CAMPAIGN

CONTENTS

1980s IMAGE GALLERY

FRONT COVER: Prime Minister Margaret Thatcher in a formal portrait taken by photographer David Montgomery inside No.10 Downing Street in 1985.

BACK COVER: The crowd at Wembley Stadium during Live Aid on 13 July, 1985.

TITLE PAGE: Teenage fans at a Duran Duran concert in the New Romantic band's home town of Birmingham, early in the decade.

OPPOSITE: Pensioners demonstrate their determination to fight for fair treatment at a rally in Parliament Square in 1981.

FOLLOWING PAGES:

A group of punks with spectacular hair take time out on a street corner in 1983.

Women at the peace camp outside RAF Greenham Common in Berkshire, protesting against the presence of cruise missiles in 1985.

An office worker in London puts across an opposing point of view to protesters on a 'Stop The City' anti-capitalist demonstration in September 1984.

Two miners return to work at Maerdy Colliery in South Wales, on 5 March, 1985, at the end of the year-long miners' strike. The last deep coal mine in the Rhondda valley, Maerdy closed the same year.

EVERYONE NEEDS STANDARDS
STANDARD
2,001,208
-and going up
Evening News
Another big rise puts the number out of work up to the highest since 1935
2,001,208
Evening News
Rule book scuppers Lionheart
Evening News
JOBLESS OVER 2 MILLION -OFFICIAL
Evening News
CITY PRICES
2,001,208 JOBLESS AND GOING UP
Evening STANDARD

THE
REVOLUTION
STALLED

There was one person who dominated Britain in the 1980s: Margaret Thatcher, the country's first woman Prime Minister. But as the decade opened, she was still finding her feet and her voice as the nation's leader. The monetarist economic policies brought in by her new Conservative government were designed to curb inflation, but the result was a steep and rapid rise in unemployment. As calls mounted for a change in policy, it was far from clear if the country was ready for the dramatic changes that Mrs Thatcher had in store.

TWO MILLION AND RISING Newspaper headlines on 27 August, 1980, proclaim the worst unemployment figures in Britain since the Great Depression of the 1930s. And they were going to get a lot worse.

THE LADY'S NOT FOR TURNING

The 1980s was one of the most radical decades of British history. It will forever be associated with Margaret Thatcher, a Prime Minister who polarised opinion like no other. Her admirers claim that she introduced a new spirit of self-reliance and enterprise; that she rolled back socialism, which she detested in all its hues, with new legislation to curb the power of the trade unions and by privatising industries, selling off council houses and lowering taxes; and that she slew the economic dragon of inflation and restored Britain's national self-confidence, not least through victory in the Falklands War. Conversely, Thatcher's detractors claim that hers was a divisive premiership that made the rich (especially in the Southeast) richer, while the poor (especially in the North) grew poorer. They blamed her hardline policies for the collapse of British industry, for an economic cycle of boom and bust, and for fostering a society in which money-making and selfishness overshadowed caring and culture.

There was one thing on which everyone did agree: Mrs Thatcher was an extraordinary character. A complex mixture of the homely, commonsense 'grocer's daughter' from Grantham and high-powered international stateswoman, she had enormous capacity for work and energy – she thrived on typically four hours of sleep a night – and a razor-sharp mind. She was courageous and ruthless, as the many ministers sacked from her cabinet could testify, yet she could draw on her femininity and the housewife image when she felt the need. Her trademark handbag, big hair and plummy voice became national icons, while her hard-nosed determination and right-wing convictions earned her the memorable sobriquet the Iron Lady (from the Russians). Less flatteringly, Denis Healey dubbed her Attila the Hen. Perhaps it was the French president François Mitterrand who best summed up her mixture of steeliness and womanly charms when he described her as having 'the eyes of Caligula, but the mouth of Marilyn Monroe'.

Wets, dries and monetarism

In its first year, Thatcher's government was very nearly wrecked on the rocks of its own economic policies. The Thatcher revolution, as it would be called, stuttered and stalled in 1980. As Prime Minister, she had not yet acquired the supreme self-confidence that would later allow her to swat her own and opposition MPs like dopey flies. She was still feeling her way, with her right-wing instincts subdued by the presence of many 'one-nation', left-of-centre, Heathite MPs in her Cabinet – those she would come to refer to disdainfully as 'wets'. They included some formidable patrician Tory figures such as Lord Carrington, Francis Pym and Willie Whitelaw. Her own more right-wing supporters were outnumbered, though they did include Sir Geoffrey Howe, who had been appointed to the key post of Chancellor.

HOLDING HER AUDIENCE
Margaret Thatcher – seen here receiving applause at the Tory Party conference at Blackpool in October 1981 – came to power at the age of 53 and held the reins for 11 years and 209 days. In that time she brought about far-reaching changes in British society. As a student she had read chemistry at Oxford then, before becoming an MP, worked as a research chemist at Lyons & Company, where she explored ways of preserving ice cream. Thatcher was not an intellectual, but she was clever and intuitive and had a genuine passion for politics. She enjoyed art, music and reading to a degree, but never seemed to relish the cultural 'hinterland' that Denis Healey felt made for a rounded person. Sir Winston Churchill was a watercolourist among other hobbies, Ted Heath had his sailing and conducting, Healey himself was a photographer and even Neil Kinnock loved his rugby. But Margaret Thatcher enjoyed nothing so much as reading civil service briefs. She was, consequently, formidably well informed, and this, coupled with a stubborn and domineering personality, enabled her to win most of the arguments both within and outside of her party.

'It will be years before a woman either leads the Conservative Party or becomes Prime Minister. I don't see it happening in my time.'

Margaret Thatcher, speaking in 1970

RISING UNEMPLOYMENT
In 1978 a famous Tory poster had shown a snaking queue of supposedly jobless people under the headline, 'Labour Isn't Working', implying that the Conservatives would reduce unemployment. But when they did get into power, unemployment rocketed. In 1981 it rose to above 13 per cent, higher than any other country in western Europe. Signing on the dole – or increasingly, as employment prospects diminished, claiming social security benefit – became the reality for thousands upon thousands of people who had never experienced unemployment before. Many young people – like this girl photographed in August 1980 – left school or college with no hope of getting a job. Thousands flocked to London looking for work, leading to a sharp rise in the number of homeless sleeping rough on the streets of the capital.

Thatcher and her closest allies – Geoffrey Howe, Keith Joseph and, at this time, John Biffen – believed that the roots of the country's economic woes lay in inflation. To tackle this they embraced monetarism, a policy championed by the Nobel-prizewinning American economist Milton Friedman, who was greatly admired by Thatcher. In short, monetarism is based on the idea that inflation comes about from too much money circulating in the economy. If governments spend more than the amount they receive in taxes, they have to compensate for the shortfall by an increase in the public-sector borrowing requirement. The consequent increase in the money supply will then push up inflation. The core monetarist belief is that governments must control the money supply by keeping a tight rein over public spending and squeezing inflation.

Sir Geoffrey Howe's budgets were to become key instruments of introducing the monetarist medicine to the public. His first, in the summer of 1979, was a mixture of public spending cuts and a switch from direct to indirect taxation. It was not long before the government and the country found that this economic tack had social consequences. As 1979 passed into 1980, the cuts in public spending deflated the economy and led to unemployment and strikes. Furthermore, the tactic of raising interest rates to cut inflation – the monetarists' preferred method – punished the mortgage-owning middle classes who made up the Tories' core constituency. To make matters even worse, Britain's North Sea Oil had elevated sterling into a petro-currency, increasing the value of the pound. This made exports more expensive and British jobs suffered. Michael Edwardes, then head of the giant state-owned car manufacturer British Leyland, actually stated at this time that the oil 'should be left in the ground'.

To turn or not to turn?

The lengthening dole queues added to the government's social security bill while reducing their income from taxes, and rising interest rates failed to curb inflation, which had been fuelled by a consumer boom resulting from tax cuts. Workers at the British Steel Corporation went on strike in January 1980 and were given a relatively generous settlement of a 16 per cent rise, with conditions. Would Thatcher lose her nerve and turn to the compromise politics she had come to despise in Ted Heath's government?

Much depended on Howe's second budget in March 1980, but it failed to stem the tide. Despite setting out a carefully crafted Medium-Term Financial Strategy designed to boost business confidence and cutting nearly £1 billion from projected public spending – social services and education both took big hits – the government watched in dismay as inflation and unemployment continued their inexorable upward spiral. By the end of 1980 the number of jobless would reach 2.8 million. By the summer of 1980, only a year into her premiership, Thatcher was under intense pressure. The crunch came at the Conservative Party conference in Brighton that October. Would she at last have a change of heart and announce a reversal of government policy? To an audience desperate for encouragement, Thatcher put her cards on the table: 'To those waiting with bated breath for that favourite media catchphrase, the U-turn, I have only one thing to say. You turn if you want to. The lady's not for turning!' Her faithful supporters reacted with cheers, and the speech was later counted as a key event in her premiership – the moment when she put clear blue water between herself and the compromise governments of the past.

JOHN LENNON – A SENSELESS DEATH

SHOT DEAD AT 40

On 9 December, 1980, Britain woke up to the news that John Lennon had been gunned down in New York. At about 11pm the previous evening, Lennon and his wife Yoko were returning to their apartment in the Dakota building opposite Central Park in Manhattan. As they walked from their car to the door, Lennon was shot four times by an unhinged 'fan' named Mark Chapman. Lennon was rushed to a local hospital, but attempts to revive him failed and he was pronounced dead on arrival. In a cruel irony, Chapman had asked Lennon for his autograph earlier in the day and the former Beatle had happily complied. As news of the shooting spread, disbelieving fans began to gather outside Lennon's home. The next day, Yoko issued a simple statement: 'John loved and prayed for the human race. Please do the same for him.' She invited people to join in a 10-minute silent vigil on the following Sunday, 14 December. An estimated 200,000 shell-shocked people gathered in Central Park (below), while back in Britain some 30,000 attended a vigil at St George's Hall in Liverpool. Tributes and memorials to John Lennon continue to this day. Chapman pleaded guilty and was sentenced to life in jail.

'Everybody loves you when you're six foot in the ground.'

John Lennon

THE YORKSHIRE RIPPER

CAUGHT AT LAST
In May 1981 one of Britain's most notorious serial killers, Peter Sutcliffe (left), was convicted of murdering 13 women and attempting to murder seven others. His terrifying spree of violence against women began in 1975 and spanned the late Seventies; two of his victims were killed in 1980. He was arrested in January 1981 and charged at the criminal court in Dewsbury, West Yorkshire, where angry crowds had to be held back by police (above). At his trial Sutcliffe denied murder, pleading guilty to manslaughter on the grounds of diminished responsibility. He claimed that he heard voices and that his killings were fulfilling God's will, but the jury found him guilty of murder on all counts. He was sentenced to life imprisonment and the judge recommended that he serve a minimum of 30 years before any consideration of parole. Sutcliffe began prison life in Parkhurst, but after three years he was moved to Broadmoor, the high-security psychiatric hospital in Berkshire. Over the years he has been attacked several times by fellow inmates, as a result of which he is now blind in one eye.

Thatcher's steely resolve gained much, often grudging, respect. But in fact she was by no means immune to compromise. In early 1981 she reluctantly agreed to bail out the floundering British Leyland. Even more galling, she gave in to the demands of the miners – Ted Heath's nemesis in 1974 – who threatened to strike over the proposed closure of 23 pits. Thatcher knew that at some stage she would have to take on the miners in a full-scale trial of strength, but she recognised that she was not yet ready. For the moment, the government agreed to reduce coal imports and give £300 million to the Coal Board.

With the government's right-wing supporters worried that it was losing its zeal, and the rest of the country dismayed and angered by its economic policies, the stage was set for Geoffrey's Howe's third budget in March 1981. It turned out to be another injection of what Denis Healey called 'sado-monetarism'. Howe froze the income tax threshold, but with inflation running at 13 per cent the measure was equivalent of a tax increase of nearly £2 billion. As the number of unemployed headed ominously towards 3 million, the ship of state seemed to be heading for the rocks. Certainly, 364 leading economists thought so, writing a joint letter to *The Times* protesting that monetarist policies would 'deepen the depression, erode the industrial base of our economy and threaten its social and political stability'. Howe would later retaliate, describing an economist as a man 'who knows 364 ways of making love, but doesn't know any women'.

OIL BONANZA
North Sea Oil workers – like these men (below) photographed on a drilling rig at Stornoway on the Isle of Lewis in the Outer Hebrides – were instrumental in making Britain a significant oil producer from the late 1970s onwards. By 1980, for the first time in its history, the country was exporting more oil than it imported and by mid-decade it was producing a peak of some 85 million barrels a month, a record at that time (production rose even further in 1999). Although it increased the value of sterling, hampering export sales, North Sea oil was credited with underpinning Britain's economy in the dark years from 1980 to 1982, when unemployment and the social security bill soared. Without it, the effects of the recession would have been even worse.

continued on page 26

RIVALRY FOR GOLD

The rivalry between middle-distance runners Steve Ovett (see page 25) and Sebastian Coe kept Olympic fans glued to their television screens and on the edge of their seats in the Moscow games. Coe was expected to win the 800 metres, with Ovett tipped for gold in the 1500, but the results turned out topsy-turvy. Coe, running what he later described as the worst tactical race of his life, could not prevent Ovett from breaking the tape first in the 800 metres final, finishing second himself. Coe was left with the 1500 metres final to redeem himself. Ovett was confident – he had not lost over that distance for three years – but Coe's performance on the day was inspired. He stormed in first (above), while Ovett took the bronze to go with his 800-metres gold.

In the pool, the bald head of Duncan Goodhew (right) was instantly recognisable and his swimming exploits were soon equally well known. Goodhew had lost his hair at the tender age of 10 and struggled at school with dyslexia, but he found an outlet for his energy in the swimming pool. His natural ability and dedication to training, including a spell at a US college, brought him success. His greatest moment came at the Moscow Olympics when he won gold in the breaststroke; he also took a bronze in the 4 x 100 metre medley relay.

BRITAIN'S 1980 OLYMPIANS

The 1980 Moscow Olympics was nearly wrecked by a US-led boycott of the games in protest over the USSR's 1979 invasion of Afghanistan. More than 60 countries followed America's lead – including West Germany, Japan and Canada – but 80 nations and 6,000 athletes did compete. Britain's athletes defied government pressure not to travel to Moscow and won 21 medals. Sebastian Coe and Steve Ovett jousted for supremacy in the 800 and 1500 metres, splitting the medal honours between them. The official poster of the games (left) featured the lines of a running track rising to form an architectural silhouette typical of the Moscow skyline.

VAULTING AMBITIONS

Daley Thompson, seen here (above) completing a pole vault in Moscow, took the gold medal in the decathlon. He finished more than 160 points ahead of his nearest rival, Yuriy Kutsenko of the USSR. Thompson was born in London of a Scottish mother and Nigerian father. His ability to excel at a number of track and field events steered him towards the decathlon. He would repeat his Olympic feat four years later, taking gold in Los Angeles in 1984.

Alan Wells (left), the powerful Scottish sprinter from Edinburgh, brought rare Olympic glory to Britain by winning gold in the iconic event of the 100 metres. The race favourite was the Cuban Silvio Leonard, but Wells dug deep to pip him at the line. He tried to repeat his success in the 200 metres but had to be content with silver, losing out to the Italian Pietro Mennea.

'Am I a failure? Is fifth place in the Olympic Games a failure? Is the best place by a British shot putter at the Olympics since 1908 failure?'

Geoff Capes

TRACK AND FIELD
'And Ovett looks up in triumph ...' were the words of the breathless BBC commentator David Coleman after Ovett upset the odds to beat Sebastian Coe and take gold in the 800 metres (above). Steve Ovett was generally perceived to have less charm and dash than Coe, but the public gradually warmed to him and relished the rivalry between the pair. Ovett was at the height of his powers in 1980 and 1981, but at the 1984 Los Angeles Olympics he was forced out of medal contention by respiratory problems.

At 6ft 5ins and 23 stones, Geoff Capes (right) was one of Britain's most memorable athletes. A former policeman, Capes had been a winning shot putter at Commonwealth, European and other games, but in Moscow he only managed fifth. As he wrote afterwards: 'I wanted to do it desperately but my body refused.'

Reshuffling the cabinet

The anger that greeted Howe's third budget seemed to find expression in a spate of riots that broke out across the country in the spring and summer of 1981 (see pages 32-40). There were some bright spots for the public that summer, notably the fairytale marriage of Prince Charles to Lady Diana Spencer and the euphoric moment when Ian Botham and the England cricket team beat Australia to win the Ashes, but even these could not camouflage a country ill at ease with itself.

Mrs Thatcher's position within her party was precarious. When, that summer, Howe declared that even more severe public spending cuts would have to be made in 1982, the Conservative 'wets' were joined in their dissent by hitherto 'dries'. A less resolute politician, or a more amenable one, would have perhaps taken more account of the disquiet of her colleagues. But Thatcher did the opposite: her answer was to surround herself with more like-minded allies. In September 1981 she made a lightning strike on her Cabinet. She sacked Ian Gilmour, Mark Carlisle and Lord Soames and moved Jim Prior to the Siberia of Northern Ireland. She then brought in more of her supporters: Norman Tebbit took Prior's old job as Employment Secretary – he would famously tell the mass unemployed to emulate his father in the Depression and get on their bikes and look for work; Nigel Lawson was moved to head up the Department of Energy; and Cecil Parkinson became Conservative Party Chairman.

The 1981 Tory Party conference in Blackpool – by now a crucial arena at which to rally the wavering – consolidated Thatcher's position. Despite a rise in interest rates to 16 per cent and opinion polls showing her government to be the least popular since the war, Thatcher reaffirmed her stand on inflation and refused to court popularity with softer policies. But her position remained tenuous. The Social Democratic Party (SDP), formed earlier in the year, were making spectacular electoral headway in alliance with the Liberal Party. On 22 October the Liberal candidate Bill Pitt won a by-election in Croydon; then, on 26 November, Shirley Williams triumphed for the SDP at Crosby. By the end of the year, Thatcher had scored the worst personal poll ratings for a Prime Minister since polls began.

But in 1982 Thatcher's fortunes and those of the government would change in spectacular fashion. Even though unemployment reached the 3 million mark in January, there were green shoots of recovery in evidence. Inflation and interest rates were falling; industrial output was improving. Thatcher declared that the country was over the worst. What she needed was an event to kickstart a new mood of optimism and growth. That event arrived in April 1982 in the unlikely form of a war thousands of miles away in the South Atlantic (see chapter 2).

THE ANTI-NUCLEAR MOVEMENT
Against a backdrop of rising Cold War tension between the USA and USSR, the anti-nuclear movement worldwide was growing rapidly in the early 1980s. In the UK, membership of CND, the Campaign for Nuclear Disarmament, rose from just over 4,000 in 1979 to 100,000 by 1984. This demonstration in London – like many others around the world at this time – was organised in 1980 in the wake of the Three Mile Island nuclear accident in the USA the previous year, which provoked a huge rise in the number of people objecting to nuclear power *per se*, not just nuclear arms.

The UK had had its own nuclear near-disaster in 1957 when fire broke out at the Windscale reactor in Cumbria (now called Sellafield). It was Britain's worst nuclear accident, discharging radioactive material for hundreds of miles around. Afterwards, the government banned milk products from cows grazing in a 200 mile-radius of the plant, but only for a period of six weeks. The accident made many in Britain profoundly uneasy about nuclear power. Michael Foot was outspoken in his anti-nuclear beliefs saying in 1960 that a Britain 'which denounced the insanity of the nuclear strategy would be in a position to direct its influence at the United Nations and in the world at large, in a manner at present denied us'. It was a commitment that Foot, as party leader, carried through into the Labour manifesto for the 1983 general election, which stated: 'The overriding task for Britain, as for the rest of the world, is to draw back from the nuclear abyss.'

LABOUR SPAWNS THE SDP

After Labour's electoral defeat in 1979, Jim Callaghan did not resign immediately as party leader. He hoped to help his favoured replacement, Denis Healey, by taking, as he said, 'some shine off the ball'. Callaghan, Healey and others on the right of the party were fighting a battle against the far left, who included members of Militant Tendency, a Trotskyist group which had been infiltrating Labour for

years. The far left wanted to impose their vision of socialism on Labour by making the leader electable by the wider party, not just by MPs, and making MPs submit themselves for reselection. They also wanted Labour's National Executive Committee to be the final arbiter on the party's manifesto, which they believed should pledge Britain to the unilateral scrapping of its nuclear deterrent and to withdrawal from the EEC. So, during 1980, the Labour Party's energy was diverted from fighting the government by its own internal struggles.

Left foot forward

Jim Callaghan finally resigned as party leader on 15 October, 1980, but to everyone's surprise he was succeeded not by Denis Healey – the bête noire of the left – but by the soft-left candidate Michael Foot, who defeated Healey in the leadership context by 139 votes to 129. A veteran campaigner for unilateral disarmament, Foot was believed to be the one person who could unite the party's warring factions. He was highly regarded by friends and foes alike as an elegant writer, an intellectual, a wit and orator, as well as a dedicated parliamentarian. Aged 67, he had a style and demeanour that evoked a bygone era when politicians mounted soap boxes with megaphones, rather than hiring PR specialists to polish up their image. The following year Healey was elected as his deputy, just managing to fight off the challenge of Tony Benn, the charismatic hero of the Left.

Foot may have been elected as a political 'healer', but Labour's wounds were wide open. On 24 January, 1981, a special party conference at Wembley confirmed that future Labour leaders (and deputy leaders) would have to be elected not just by MPs but by an electoral college consisting of MPs (30 per cent), party activists (30 per cent) and – much to the dismay of Labour right-wingers – trade unions, who were granted 40 per cent of the vote. It was a significant victory for Tony Benn and his comrades. For a clutch of former Labour cabinet ministers this formalised lurch to the left was the straw that broke the camel's back.

DREAM ON
The left wing of the Labour Party seemed to be in the ascendant when Michael Foot (above, on the left) beat Denis Healey in the leadership election. Having first entered Parliament in 1945, Foot was acclaimed for his parliamentary oratory and brought a wealth of experience to the role of Labour Party leader. He lost out to Jim Callaghan in the leadership election in 1975, but served in the Callaghan administration as Employment Secretary and leader of the House of Commons. Foot was no friend of the Militant Tendency, the far left group championed by Tony Benn (above right), but he nevertheless declared to journalists after his election that 'I am as strong in my socialist convictions as I have ever been'. These included a long-held unilateralist disarmament stance on nuclear weapons, which many of his senior party colleagues – although not Tony Benn – found hard to agree with. Benn's best chance of advancement in the post-Callaghan Labour Party was as deputy leader to Foot, but in September 1981 he lost out to Healey by 10 votes: 'Healey – by an eyebrow', the *Daily Mirror* cheekily declared (Healey had particularly bushy eyebrows, a physical characteristic latched onto by cartoonists).

TRYING TO BREAK THE MOULD

Three members of the so-called 'gang of four' (right) – from the left, Roy Jenkins, Bill Rodgers and Dr David Owen – who along with Shirley Williams formally launched the Social Democratic Party (SDP) in the spring of 1981. Their aim was to woo moderates from both the Labour and Conservative parties in order to break the two-party mould of British politics. The possibility of a new political party had been in the air for a year or so. A key moment came in November 1979 when Roy Jenkins, then still President of the European Commission, gave the Richard Dimbleby Lecture which he titled 'Home Thoughts from Abroad'. He spoke of the 'constricting rigidity' of the 'party system' and the idea of a 'radical centre', and the positive public response he received may have convinced him that a new party was feasible. Within 16 months the SDP was a reality. The new party joined forces with the Liberals in autumn 1981, an alliance embraced by delegates at the Liberal Party conference in Llandudno that September (below).

'When our alliance
government takes office, it will
represent the last, best hope
of the British people.'

David Steel, speaking at the Liberal Party Conference at Llandudno, September 1981

The gang of four

The very next day, 25 January, 1981, Shirley Williams, Roy Jenkins (both without parliamentary seats, Williams having been defeated in the 1979 election, while Jenkins had been serving as President of the European Commission), Bill Rodgers and David Owen published the Limehouse Declaration, named after Limehouse in East London, where Owen lived. The declaration referred to the 'calamitous outcome' of the Labour Party conference and the fact that a 'handful of trade union leaders can now dictate the choice of a future prime minister'. It proposed a new 'council for social democracy' and set out ideals that steered a course between the Labour left and Tory right: 'We want to eliminate poverty and promote greater equality without stifling enterprise or imposing bureaucracy from the centre.' The declaration was the founding document of the Social Democratic Party (SDP).

On 26 March, some 500 journalists squeezed into the Connaught Rooms in Covent Garden to see the 'gang of four' formally launch the SDP. Sitting side by side before a backdrop of smart red-and-blue SDP logos, the four politicians appealed for new supporters and declared their aspiration to break the political mould. Pledging to overhaul the system, fight for equal rights for women and ethnic groups, and to implement a more equitable distribution of wealth, the four pioneers emphasised their aim of healing class divisions and reconciling the nation.

Their message fell on eager ears. Before long the SDP bandwagon was rolling. Thirteen Labour MPs and one Conservative (Christopher Brocklebank-Fowler) were to join them, and thousands of people, mostly from the professional middle classes, sent messages of support. Lord Sainsbury was among the wealthy backers who donated money. Media interest was intense and SDP meetings were packed.

The first true test of support was not long in coming. In a by-election held on 16 July, 1981, Roy Jenkins contested the safe Labour seat of Warrington and came within a couple of thousand votes of beating the Labour candidate Doug Hoyle. Afterwards Jenkins declared to the press that although it was the first time in 30 years of politics that he had been defeated, it was 'by far the greatest victory I have participated in'. In the autumn, an agreement between the SDP and the Liberals to form an alliance was ratified by the Liberals at their conference in Llandudno. Shirley Williams and Roy Jenkins were warmly welcomed as they addressed fringe meetings and in an atmosphere of euphoria David Steel famously jumped the electoral gun with his much-quoted rallying call to the party faithful: 'Go back to your constituencies and prepare for government.'

But the close result at Warrington showed that the SDP could muster support. Shirley Williams' victory at the Crosby by-election on 26 November, followed by Roy Jenkins' by-election triumph at Glasgow Hillhead on 25 March, 1982, confirmed it. Could the SDP-Liberal alliance break the mould of British politics?

TWO-TONE SKA

In the summer of 1981 the Specials captured the mood of a nation racked by factory closures and unemployment with their atmospheric and lyrical 'Ghost Town'. Fronted by vocalist Terry Hall – seen here wearing his trademark shades – the band formed in Coventry in the late Seventies, drawing inspiration from the Rock against Racism movement pioneered by bands such as the Clash. Their sound combined Jamaican ska with British punk and in 1979 they scored a first top 10 hit with 'Gangsters', followed in 1980 with 'Too Much Too Young' which went all the way to number one. 'Ghost Town' consolidated their success and provided the soundtrack to race riots and a royal wedding. The band are shown here playing at The Hope and Anchor, a large Victorian pub in Islington that hosted gigs from the mid-Seventies onwards. Its dank basement lent the right atmosphere to the punk, new wave and ska bands that pulled in the music fans.

WRITING ON THE WALL

The riots that broke out across the country in spring 1981 shook the country to its core. Night after night, grim-faced television reporters updated the nation on the latest violence against a backdrop of flaming buildings, burnt-out cars, battered streets and lines of shield-bearing policemen.

Unemployment, racism and policing were thought to be the triple-headed cause for the violent disturbances.

As the graffiti above indicates, there had been a warning the previous spring of what might happen when rioting broke out in the St Pauls area of Bristol, after police raided a café frequented mainly by black youths.

Racial tensions in London were stoked further following a house fire in New Cross in the early hours of Sunday, 18 January, 1981. Thirteen black teenagers who had been celebrating a joint birthday party died in the tragedy. The victims' families and other local residents believed the police were tardy and unsympathetic in their

ANGER, RIOTING AND RACE

In June 1981, the Coventry-based ska band the Specials released 'Ghost Town', a bleak, haunting song that climbed to the top of the singles charts on 11 July and stayed there for three weeks. The song seemed to capture perfectly the spirit of the times and the state of the country, with lyrics reflecting the dire unemployment and sense of despair that lay behind the outbreaks of rioting spreading like a virus through the major cities of the land in the spring and summer of 1981. Deprived urban areas witnessed scenes of civic violence not seen since Victorian times. Brixton, Southall and Battersea in London, Handsworth in Birmingham, Chapeltown in Leeds, Highfields in Leicester, Manchester's Moss Side and Toxteth in Liverpool were just some of the places that echoed to the sounds of smashed windows and the flickering shadows of burning cars.

Although the riots lasted only a few months, dying out almost as quickly as they sprang to life, their ferocity and extensiveness shook the government. The violence was blamed by the rioters and left-wing commentators on poverty, the lack of jobs, and a sense of injustice and alienation. There was also a racial factor. Policing in areas with sizeable black populations was already a sensitive issue

investigation of the case. On 2 March, an estimated 10,000 to 15,000 people joined grieving relatives to march from New Cross to the House of Commons demanding justice (right). They believed that arson was involved, but the coroner recorded an open verdict, a decision that has since been upheld in response to later challenges.

BRIXTON IN FLAMES
From 10 to 13 April, 1981, Brixton in south London became the scene of the first serious rioting in Britain in the 20th century. At the SDP launch some two weeks earlier, Roy Jenkins had enthused about releasing 'the energies of people' disenchanted with the political stalemate. But the SDP was no conduit for the 'energies' of disenchanted black youths in Brixton, whose frustration at insensitive policing and discrimination erupted in violence (left). Police struggled to contain the riots with baton charges and defensive formations (below); it was later said the experience served the police well for the miners' strike in 1984.

Unemployment certainly did not help the issue. Some on the left of the Tory Party, including Jim Prior and Sir Ian Gilmour, had warned that the government's perceived indifference towards the unemployed might result in widespread disorder. Mrs Thatcher, on the other hand, saw the riots in Brixton and elsewhere in terms of law and order. She was more interested in prosecution for the 'criminals' than investigating underlying grievances, although her Home Secretary did instigate an inquiry by Lord Scarman.

when, on 13 January, 1981, a fire at a house in New Cross, south London, claimed the lives of 13 young black people who had been enjoying a birthday party. Although the police mounted a major investigation, black community leaders believed that they and the media were not taking the case as seriously as they would if the victims had been white. On 2 March a 'Black People's Day of Action' saw up to 15,000 march from the borough of Lewisham to central London bearing placards with the words, 'Thirteen Dead, Nothing Said'.

Losing control in Brixton

At the beginning of April, the police began a stop-and-search operation in Brixton, south London, under the so-called 'sus' laws which gave officers the right to arrest anyone they believed to be acting suspiciously. The operation was codenamed 'Swamp', seemingly after a comment Margaret Thatcher had made in January 1978 to the effect that 'People are really rather afraid that this country might be rather swamped by people of a different culture'. During a week's work, more than a hundred plain-clothes officers stopped nearly a thousand people in Brixton, the overwhelming majority of them young blacks. Resentment and tension mounted and on 10 April a clash occurred between the police and black youths. Ironically, it was sparked by police attempting to help a young black man who had been stabbed. Rumour and misunderstanding abounded, and the following day, as the police resumed Operation Swamp, a full-scale riot ensued. In the evening, rioters – who included white youths – burned cars, smashed windows, looted shops and threw bricks, bottles and petrol bombs at the police.

After three days of rioting, some 300 policemen and more than 60 civilians were injured. In the aftermath, the government set up an inquiry under Lord Scarman, which would lead to a change in some elements of policing, notably the scrapping of the hated 'sus' law which was found to be at least in part to blame. The report also to led to the establishment of the Police Complaints Authority.

Anger in the north

Nearly three months after Brixton it was the turn of Liverpool to feel the full force of rioters. On 5 July, the deprived area of Toxteth erupted into flames. A couple of hundred white and black youths hurled bricks, bits of scaffolding and petrol bombs at shops and police, who were equipped with riot shields. Victims included a BBC camera crew who fled before a gang armed with pick-axe handles, losing

VIEWING THE DAMAGE
When the rioting in Brixton was at its height, firemen could not reach some of the blazing buildings to douse the flames. Many properties, including a post office, a school and an off-licence were burnt out. One local landmark that went up in flames was the Windsor Castle pub in Leeson Road. In all some 30 buildings were destroyed by fire, with another 120 badly damaged. About 100 cars and vans were burned, including more than 50 police vehicles.

continued on page 40

LIVERPOOL ALIGHT

On 4 July, 1981, it was the turn of Toxteth in central Liverpool to undergo the ordeal of rioting. As *The Times* reported, 'Buildings blazed as the rioters, some little more than children, attacked police with barrages of missiles, driving hijacked milk-floats and a concrete-mixer into their midst.' The mayhem continued for nine days, leaving the streets scarred with charred and blackened buildings (below). Merseyside police had to draft in reinforcements from other regions to help them regain control. In an ugly footnote to the riots, on 17 August, a month after the original riot petered out, an anti-police demonstration turned to violence (right). Mrs Thatcher's reaction to events in Toxteth was to identify with those whose property had been damaged – her instinctive cry was: 'Oh, those poor shopkeepers!' Although she asserted that unemployment was not the main factor in causing the riots, Toxteth had one of the highest unemployment rates in the country.

CARNIVAL TIME

ALL SMILES

Having swapped hats with the lady, a policeman sweeps her up in his arms during London's Notting Hill Carnival on 31 August, 1981. The photograph recorded a welcome cameo of good humour just four months after the riots in Brixton. The Carnival celebrated black, specifically West Indian, culture in Britain and it now became a beacon of hope in the midst of troubled race relations, attracting hundreds of thousands of people of all shades every year with its colourful floats and processions, calypso and samba, steel bands and reggae.

Notting Hill Carnival had first become established as an institution in the 1960s and it came to act as an unofficial barometer of racial tension in London. Recent events in Brixton, as well as riots at the Carnival itself back in 1976, encouraged a radical rethink of policing policy. The Carnival was a good public platform on which the police could demonstrate a more sympathetic, hearts-and-minds approach to community relations. In 1984 the police went beyond a friendly approach on the day by sending the Metropolitan Police Brass Band to perform from an open-topped bus festooned with balloons. The band was well received, but old habits on both sides did not change so easily overnight. Insensitive policing continued in the 1980s and tensions at the Carnival never fully disappeared, breaking out again in serious violence in 1987 when a member of the public was murdered.

their £12,000 camera in the process. As in Brixton, relations between the police and the local community in Toxteth were severely strained, with huge resentment at heavy-handed policing and the 'sus' law. The initial violence was sparked by an attempt to arrest a young black man on Friday, 3 July, but as the riots took hold that weekend they involved as many disaffected white youths as black. In the street battles that ensued, the police used CS gas for the first time in a civil disturbance on mainland Britain and reinforcements had to be called in from other regions. By the time the riots had petered out nine days later, 468 policemen had been injured and some 500 people arrested. More than 100 buildings had been burnt out, many of them so badly damaged they had to be pulled down.

The civic unrest continued across the country throughout July. Moss Side in Manchester was the next major flashpoint, when some 1,000 people besieged the local police station on 8 July. The rioting lasted for 48 hours, during which time Moss Side saw its share of arson and looting.

The political reaction

The government was rattled. Willie Whitelaw, then Thatcher herself, visited Toxteth in the immediate aftermath. Environment Secretary Michael Heseltine also made a high-profile visit. He had been responsible for the government's generally popular Housing Act of 1980, which allowed council tenants the right to buy their houses or flats at a reduced percentage of the market price. Identified with the liberal, more caring side of Toryism, and a dynamic, brilliant communicator, Heseltine was the best person the government had to pour oil on troubled waters. He stayed in Liverpool for three weeks and in the end 'Mr Merseyside', as he was dubbed, banged local business heads together, cut through red tape and injected some much needed investment and a sense of new purpose into the city.

In the House of Commons the Prime Minister was taken to task by the leaders of the Opposition over the worst rioting that Britain had seen in the entire 20th century. She defended herself with vigour and although on 14 July she conceded that unemployment was a factor in the violence, she went on to say: 'I do not believe that it is the main factor. Some of the worst riots occurred in areas where unemployment was far from being as high as in other areas.' In fact, Toxteth had a particularly high level of unemployment, partly as a long-term legacy of the decline in the docks. Two days later, Mrs Thatcher declared: 'Society must have rules if it is to continue to be civilised. Those rules must be observed and upheld by Government and by all leaders throughout the community.'

By the end of the month the rioting fever had more or less run its course. Whether the marriage of Prince Charles to Lady Diana Spencer on 29 July cast a romantic spell that defused the tension, it is hard to tell, but certainly the wedding was a major and welcome distraction to millions of Britons.

STRIKING TO DEATH

The IRA hunger striker Bobby Sands (right), who died on 5 May, 1981, after two months without food. He was buried two days later in Belfast. The funeral party included IRA members in combat jackets, masks and berets, as well as members of Sands' family (bottom right). The Prime Minister had taken an unflinching stand against the hunger strikers. For her they were criminals who did not deserve special status as prisoners. 'The Government', she declared, 'is not prepared to legitimise their cause by word or deed'. But her victory, if such it was, was a pyrrhic one. Posters of Bobby Sands became ubiquitous – at the time, almost as iconic as those of Che Guevara in the 1960s and 70s – and donations from the IRA's American sympathisers increased as a result of the publicity. And more than 70 civilians, police and soldiers were killed in violence directly associated with the hunger strike, including a nail bomb detonated by the IRA near Chelsea Barracks that maimed 40 people, mostly soldiers, and killed two passers-by.

'Alone, every night ... I would stand with a glass of wine, looking out at the magnificent view over the river, and ask myself what had gone wrong for this great English city.'

Michael Heseltine, on trying to understand the causes of the Toxteth riots in Liverpool

THE IRA HUNGER STRIKERS

While rioters on mainland Britain protested against poverty, unemployment and racial discrimination, another group of protesters was mounting a smaller-scale but no less effective campaign in Northern Ireland. In the Maze Prison near Belfast a number of convicted IRA men went on hunger strike from March 1981 demanding the right to be treated as political prisoners. By the time the strike was called off in October of that year, ten men had starved themselves to death. Margaret Thatcher claimed victory in not succumbing to their demands, but the hunger strike was widely seen as a propaganda triumph for the IRA and Sinn Fein, their political masters, since world opinion tended to condemn the British government for not doing more to avert the deaths.

The hunger strikes were the climax of a protest that went back to 1976. In that year, the British government took away the Special Category Status of IRA inmates, which had in effect recognised them as prisoners of war rather than ordinary criminals and had given them certain privileges, such as wearing civilian clothes and not doing prison work. When the special status privileges were withdrawn, IRA prisoners protested by refusing to wear prison clothes. Later they

started their dirty protest of smearing excrement on the walls of their cells. In October 1980, seven prisoners embarked on the ultimate protest, mounting a hunger strike until apparent concessions from the government persuaded them to call it off in December. The following year, with the prisoners still unhappy about their status and conditions, a second hunger strike was initiated.

The first man to go on hunger strike was Bobby Sands on 1 March. At first, publicity surrounding his action was relatively muted, but that changed dramatically in April when Sands stood as a candidate in the by-election for Fermanagh and South Tyrone held on 9 April. He won both the seat and a huge propaganda coup for the IRA. World attention only grew as Sands himself grew weaker. He died of starvation on 5 May, 1981.

After Sands died, the Northern Ireland Secretary of the day, Humphrey Atkins, issued a statement expressing his regret for a 'needless and pointless death'. But the other IRA hunger strikers were undeterred. Nine more men would die from lack of food before the strike was called off on 3 October, 1981. In the end, it was pressure from the strikers' families and the Catholic Church, as well as concessions wrung from Jim Prior, the new Northern Ireland Secretary, that halted the campaign. The government, meanwhile, had introduced legislation to stop other long-term prisoners being nominated as election candidates.

FOREIGN AFFAIRS

By the end of Margaret Thatcher's reign as Prime Minister in 1990, the Berlin Wall had fallen and the Soviet Union had lost a large clump of its satellite countries, including East Germany, Czechoslovakia and Poland, to Western-style democracy. The Cold War was officially declared over. But global affairs were very different when Thatcher first assumed power. The USA and the Soviet Union, together with their respective allies, were engaged in a titanic ideological struggle, both jealously guarding their regional spheres of influence. In December 1979 the Soviets ratcheted up the tension when they invaded Afghanistan to support the country's communist government. In a symbolic response, Mrs Thatcher tried to follow the lead set by the USA and boycott the Moscow Olympics, but she could not prevent Britain's athletes from competing. More tellingly, in the early 1980s NATO began to deploy new missiles to counteract the Soviet threat, provoking massive CND demonstrations across western Europe.

Mrs Thatcher, already dubbed the Iron Lady by the Soviets following an anti-communist speech she made in 1977, would become a leading protagonist in the Cold War. In particular, her strong, warm relationship with President Ronald Reagan – who replaced Jimmy Carter as head of the free world in January 1981 – was key, many believe, to winning that struggle.

Over the years, Mrs Thatcher grew to become an important figure on the world stage. She took a deep interest in the Middle East and the conflict between

A SPECIAL RELATIONSHIP
When Ronald Reagan became president of the USA in 1981 he soon found a friend and ally in Margaret Thatcher – to a degree that might perhaps have surprised them both. Reagan, here sitting next to Thatcher at a British embassy dinner in Washington DC in February 1981, was an ex-Hollywood actor and a people person, better on the big picture than the detail, which he left for others to figure out. Non-academic and non-intellectual, he was nevertheless shrewd and engaging, charming people with his self-deprecating humour. In many ways Thatcher could not have been more different: nobody ever accused her of having a sense of humour, and she very much thrived on detail and the cut-and-thrust of argument. But the chemistry between the two genuinely worked, and they brought out the best in each other. They shared a common purpose in the fight against communism and socialism, promoting right-wing political and economic values. With Pope John Paul II, they are credited by some for the West's victory in the Cold War. Mrs Thatcher herself was in no doubt about President Reagan's part in that victory. On his death in 2004 she issued a statement which included the following tribute: 'Ronald Reagan had a higher claim than any other leader to have won the Cold War for liberty and he did it without a shot being fired. To have achieved so much against so many odds and with such humour and humanity made Ronald Reagan a truly great American hero.'

'President Reagan was one of my closest political and dearest personal friends.'

Margaret Thatcher, speaking of Ronald Reagan on his death in June 2004

Israel and its Arab neighbours. She oversaw the transformation of Rhodesia into Zimbabwe, with a black government. And although she would later be perceived as a die-hard Eurosceptic, she threw herself into the affairs of the EEC.

Iranian crises

The Middle East was especially tense during Thatcher's first two years of government. In 1979 the Iranian revolution overthrew the Shah and brought to power the passionately anti-Western cleric, Ayatollah Khomeini. The following year saw the start of the bitter eight-year war between Iran and Iraq, with the West supporting and supplying Sadam Hussein's Iraq. In November 1979, militant supporters of Khomeini stormed the US embassy in Tehran and took 90 hostages. The hostage crisis dominated America and also gave Mrs Thatcher the chance to reaffirm Britain's 'special relationship' with the country. On a visit to Washington that December to meet President Carter, she reassured and delighted her hosts: 'At times like these you are entitled to look to your friends for support. We are your friends, we do support you.' On 24 April, 1980, the Americans tried to free the hostages by force, but the attempt failed dismally.

On 30 April, Britain was faced with its own embassy crisis when a group of six armed Iranians opposed to Khomeini's government seized the Iranian embassy in London, taking 26 hostages. They demanded the release of political prisoners held in Iran and freedom for the province of Khuzestan in the south of the country. The tension grew over the following days until the gunmen shot dead one of the

THE SAS GO INTO ACTION

On 5 May, 1980, the SAS stormed the Iranian embassy in London with the aim of freeing the hostages held inside. As shots rang out and fire started in the building, journalist Sim Harris – one of two BBC men who had been caught up in the crisis – made his escape across the balcony (below). The SAS operation was meticulous in its execution, as four-man teams entered from various vantage points. In 15 minutes it was all over and 19 hostages were led to safety. One hostage was shot dead by one of the gunmen during the operation, bringing the total number of hostages killed to two. Four hostages had been released during the previous few days. Five of the six gunmen were shot dead by the SAS; one was taken prisoner and later jailed. PC Trevor Lock, who had been on duty as the police guard at the embassy when the siege began, was later awarded the George Medal for his brave conduct while held prisoner and for tackling the leader of the gunmen as the SAS stormed in.

hostages, an Iranian press attaché, and threw his body unceremoniously out into the street. Fearing more bloodshed, the Home Secretary Willie Whitelaw authorised the SAS to go in. With television cameras recording the action – millions watched the events as they unfolded – the masked troopers broke into the building from the balcony and through both back and front doors, throwing stun grenades inside. In just 15 minutes the operation was over and most of the hostages were freed unharmed; five of the six gunmen lay dead. The operation launched the SAS into the limelight, turning them from a low-key shadowy force into heroes and in the process ensuring the future survival of the regiment.

From Rhodesia to Zimbabwe

Compared with the situation in Iran and the Middle East, the change that transformed white-ruled Rhodesia into black-ruled Zimbabwe was relatively smooth, and the British government made a significant contribution to the changeover. Back in 1965 Ian Smith, Rhodesia's white prime minister, had proclaimed UDI – a Unilateral Declaration of Independence – in order to maintain the white minority's grip on power in the country. The declaration brought opprobrium and sanctions from Britain and most of the rest of the world, but it was the constant guerrilla warfare led by Robert Mugabe and Joshua Nkomo that took the greatest toll on the Smith government. By the late Seventies they had been forced to the negotiating table. In 1978 Smith promised support for a black government, but one led by the moderate Bishop Abel Muzorewa. The proposed arrangement would allow whites to keep their positions in the security forces,

FORCES ON PARADE
The Queen Mother photographed with members of the Irish Guards on St Patrick's Day, 17 March, 1981, after presenting them with the traditional shamrock. The Guards and other members of Britain's armed forces suffered anxious times at the start of the 1980s, with the ever-present threat of financial cuts hanging over them. But two things helped to raise the military's profile and therefore support its interests: the emergence of the SAS as a headline-grabbing, counter-insurgency unit; and the Falklands War in 1982, which saw a national mobilisation of military force not witnessed since the Second World War.

The Irish Guards were formed in 1900 and became affectionately known as 'the Micks'. They have an Irish wolfhound as their mascot and on St Patrick's Day they are presented with fresh sprigs of shamrock, traditionally by a member of the Royal family. The Queen Mother performed this duty for several decades, and her affection for the Guards was commemorated at her funeral in 2002, when eight members of the battalion carried her coffin.

civil service and other key institutions, but the compromise failed to convince anyone and Smith and Muzorewa were eventually pressurised into meeting Mugabe and Nkomo at a conference in London in the autumn of 1979. The delegates agreed on a ceasefire, a new constitution and interim arrangements until elections could be held. Lord Soames became temporary governor with the task of enforcing law and order and ensuring that the elections were fair.

The elections duly took place on 4 March, 1980, and Mugabe won easily to become Zimbabwe's first black prime minister. The result was hailed as a great success and it boosted Britain's standing among developing nations, as Mugabe began his premiership in an atmosphere of great optimism. But the honeymoon soon ended. Faction fighting, land-distribution issues, government corruption, mismanagement and human rights abuses, drought, famine, debt and AIDS would reduce the country from one of Africa's richest to one of the poorest, an ugly blot on Britain's post-colonial record.

Europe and the British rebate

Mrs Thatcher had an uneasy relationship with the European Community. She disliked the innate corporatism of the EEC, with its enthusiasm for legislation and a lumbering bureaucracy that produced 'wine lakes' and 'butter mountains'. Yet unlike the official position of the Labour Party in the early 1980s, she had no wish to leave the community. She was, however, determined to fight Britain's corner.

When she arrived on the European scene in 1979, Thatcher faced two main problems. The first was that the experienced French and German premiers, Valéry Giscard-d'Estaing and Helmut Schmidt, saw her as the junior partner. The second was the size of the British contribution to the annual European budget. At the European Council in Dublin in November 1979, she made no bones about demanding a £1 billion rebate for Britain. She was offered £350 million, which she summarily rejected. She brow-beat the other leaders throughout an epic four-hour dinner, insisting on the return of 'our money'. Schmidt pretended to fall asleep through her harangue, while Giscard buried his head in a newspaper. It was agreed that discussions should continue in Luxembourg in April 1980.

Luxembourg seem to hold out more hope for a settlement. The Europeans offered Britain a £700 million rebate with an increase over a period of two years. But to everyone's amazement Mrs Thatcher rejected this offer, too. She still insisted on the full repayment. Next came a meeting of the Council of Ministers in Brussels in May. This time she left her ministers, Lord Carrington and Sir Ian Gilmour, to continue the fight. After hard discussions they came away with an interim deal that more or less mirrored what had been offered in Luxembourg. When they reported back to her at Chequers, she was reportedly 'incandescent' and dressed them down for a couple of hours. But it was too late. The newspapers got wind of the deal, and, ironically, praised Thatcher for defending Britain's interests so well.

Thatcher was perceived to have won the battle of the rebate, but victory turned out to be a double-edged sword. Her unbending manner had made her, and Britain, no friends among the Europeans. Although she formed better relationships with Schmidt's and Giscard's successors, Helmut Kohl and François Mitterrand, towards the end of the decade her instinctive negative attitude towards Europe hardened. Her patriotism could easily slide into anti-European rhetoric, which amplified by the tabloids was absorbed by many ordinary Britons. It also stoked divisions over Europe that would haunt the Conservative Party for years to come.

GETTING TO KNOW THE NEIGHBOURS
Thatcher's first foreign visit as Prime Minister, in June 1979, was to meet Valéry Giscard-d'Estaing, the patrician French president. They seemed to strike a cordial note; after the meeting she sent him a warm letter, thanking him profusely for a 'magnificent gift' of Sevres porcelain. But the relationship was to undergo constant strain because of her dogged insistence that Britain's budget contribution to the EEC should be reduced and Britain be paid a rebate. This photograph of the two together (top right) was taken at a press conference on 20 September, 1980.

The rebate issue also strained Thatcher's relationship with Helmut Schmidt, who was West German chancellor when she came to power. The situation improved with Schmidt's successor, Helmut Kohl, a large, plain-speaking man who came to power in October 1982. Kohl and Thatcher are seen here (bottom right) in amiable mood at a press conference in Downing Street in April 1983. But over the decade her relations with Kohl, too, deteriorated – predictably over the European project, but also over the reunification of Germany. In his memoirs, Kohl lamented that 'Margaret Thatcher always gave me headaches'.

FANCY DRESS
Diana stole the show with her 'meringue' wedding dress, its sweeping 25-foot train creating a gentle stream of ivory in her wake. In the words of Suzy Menkes, fashion correspondent of *The Times*: 'A gentle flounce of ivory taffeta, overlaid with a second tier of pearl-encrusted lace, framed her sweet young face and long neck.' The dress was the creation of David and Elizabeth Emmanuel and valued at almost £10,000. Prince Charles wore his dress naval uniform, while the Queen's wedding outfit was in pale aquamarine. Dr Robert Runcie, the Archbishop of Canterbury, performed the marriage ceremony, in which both the bride and bridegroom stumbled slightly over their words.

THE FAIRYTALE WEDDING

In what was thought by some to be the wedding of the century, Prince Charles, heir to the British throne, married Lady Diana Spencer on 29 July, 1981. Some 750 million people around the world turned on their TV sets to watch the 'fairytale' unfold in the elegant setting of Sir Christopher Wren's St Paul's Cathedral. For most people, the wedding was a welcome splash of colour in a summer dominated by riots and rising unemployment. Charles and Diana were set to be the future king and queen, as proclaimed on the banner (below) lofted high above the crowds in London. As it turned out the royal couple divorced in 1996.

FROM ENGAGEMENT TO HONEYMOON

From the moment that Lady Diana was revealed as the possible fiancée of Prince Charles, the British press could not get enough of her. The first photographs of the naive 19 year old showed her with some of the children at the London nursery where she worked, the sun behind her turning her light summer skirt see-through. That naivety can still be seen in this photo taken at Balmoral in May 1981 (left), three months after the engagement was announced in February. Although certainly pretty, there is little in her demeanour to indicate her subsequent transformation into one of the world's most beautiful women.

Immediately after the wedding in St Paul's, Charles and Diana returned to Buckingham Palace and delighted the crowds by kissing on the balcony. Later, they travelled by train down to the Broadlands estate in Hampshire, once home of the late Earl Mountbatten, Charles's much-loved great-uncle, who was killed by an IRA bomb in 1979. Queen Elizabeth and Prince Philip had also honeymooned there in 1947. The honeymoon continued with a cruise of the Mediterranean in the royal yacht *Britannia*; stopping off points included a gaily festooned Malta (right). They rounded off the holiday with a stay at Balmoral. The couple wasted no time in starting a family. Diana gave birth to William on 21 June, 1982; Harry was born on 15 September, 1984.

VICTORY IN THE ASHES

BOTHAM'S FINEST HOUR

The Ashes Test series between England and Australia in 1981 created the legend of Ian Botham. The burly England all-rounder performed such heroics on the field that he spellbound the country. The series started off with an Australian win at Trent Bridge and a draw at Lords. In the third Test at Headingley, Leeds, Australia were on course to win handsomely. They made England follow on, and an innings defeat looked likely. Then Botham came in to bat and scored an inspired 149 not out, ably assisted by the tail-enders, managing to set Australia a target of 130 runs. Australia still seemed on course to win, but Bob Willis, England's tall, bushy-haired paceman, bowled like a man possessed taking 8 wickets for just 43 runs as England skittled the Aussies out for 111.

With the series all square, the fourth Test at Edgbaston in Birmingham proved to be a low-scoring game. Australia appeared to be coming out on top, needing just 46 runs to regain a series lead, when Botham, a medium-fast, right-arm seamer, conjured more magic. He took five wickets in quick succession to wrap up the match, returning extraordinary bowling figures for the innings of 5 for 11. Next, at Old Trafford, Botham scored another century and England came out the winners by 103 runs. The final Test, at the Oval, ended on 1 September in a draw, and Botham was again the star taking 10 wickets in the match.

In this scene from the Edgbaston game, a jubilant Botham has just caught the Australian batsman Graham Yallop off the bowling of John Emburey. Bob Taylor is the wicketkeeper and Mike Gatting is in the slips to the right. Mike Brearley, England's captain, stands behind Botham.

ENEMIES WITHOUT AND WITHIN

When Britain and Argentina went to war over the Falklands, the Argentinian writer Jorge Luis Borges memorably likened the dispute to two bald men fighting over a comb. But the conflict had deeper implications than Borges's comic image suggests. In Argentina it led to the demise of Colonel Galtieri, the head of the military junta who had authorised the invasion, and paved the way for a return to civilian rule. In contrast, in Britain it spectacularly revived the fortunes of Mrs Thatcher and her Conservative government.

WELCOME HOME A British soldier is reunited with his family on 30 July, 1982. Not everyone was lucky enough to return from the Falklands War. The 74-day campaign took the lives of 252 British servicemen and three women.

THE FALKLANDS WAR

The voice of Governor Rex Hunt was heard on Falklands radio at 7.30pm on 1 April, 1982, addressing the 1,800 British-descended inhabitants of the Falkland Islands. 'I shall come on the air again as soon as I have anything to report. But in the meantime I would urge you all to remain calm, and to stay off the streets. In particular, do not go along the Airport Road. Stay indoors, and please do not add to the troubles of the security services by making demonstrations or damaging Argentine property.' The tone has the eerie feel of a 1940s BBC wartime broadcast, which seems fitting for the events unfolding in this remote and wind-swept remnant of imperial times. The next day the Argentine forces invaded and took control of the islands. The Falklands War had begun.

Argentina invades Las Malvinas

The war itself was precipitated by turbulence in Argentina. By the late 1970s, the military junta in control of Argentina was struggling to hold on to power in the face of widespread civil unrest. In 1981 General Leopoldo Galtieri became the leader of a new junta and soon authorised a plan to invade the Falklands, hoping to take the minds of the Argentinian public off their economic and social woes. Argentina had always laid claim to the Falklands, which they call Las Malvinas, on the basis of geographical proximity: the islands lie in the South Atlantic about 300 miles east of the country.

By late March 1982 the British government was convinced that Argentina was about to invade. But despite a diplomatic intervention by President Reagan, made at the request of Mrs Thatcher, they were unable to stop the invasion taking place. As Argentine forces began their landings on 2 April, Rex Hunt was heard to remark, 'It looks as though the silly buggers mean it'. The 80 Royal Marines who had taken up positions in the capital of Port Stanley were hopelessly outnumbered by 3,000 Argentinian troops. After a few hours Hunt ordered the Marines to surrender.

The next day the United Nations passed a resolution calling for hostilities to cease, for Argentina to withdraw its troops, and for Britain and Argentina to negotiate over sovereignty. Meanwhile, Mrs Thatcher was telling a hushed House of Commons that Britain would send a military task force within 48 hours to retake the islands – a plan of action supported by Opposition leader Michael Foot (who later called for a diplomatic solution) and by David Owen of the SDP. So, on 5 April, the Royal Navy's two giant aircraft carriers, *Hermes* and *Invincible*, sailed out of Portsmouth at the head of a fleet of more than a hundred ships carrying around 27,000 service personnel. Bands played, flags were waved, and a tide of popular jingoism was unleashed against the 'Argies'.

> 'This is British territory. You're not invited. We don't want you here. I want you to go now and take all your men with you.'
>
> Falklands governor Sir Rex Hunt to Argentine Admiral Carlos Busser

INVASION FORCE
Weighed down by their gear, Argentine soldiers arrive on the Falklands prepared for a lengthy stay (below). Some clearly enjoyed the idea of buying postcards to send to friends and family back home. From their relaxed and smiling faces, it does not look like they expected their invasion to be challenged militarily. The sovereignty of the Falkland Islands, along with that of South Georgia, an uninhabited island dependency lying 800 miles further east, had been disputed by Argentina since the 17th century. Britain declared the Falklands a colony in 1833, and by 1982 there were some 1,800 people of British descent living there, with thousands of sheep and not much else. At the time many asked why risk lives on re-taking the islands? But Mrs Thatcher never hesitated from the principle that British sovereignty could not be allowed to be overturned by force.

HEADING SOUTH

Britain's task force was spearheaded by two giant aircraft carriers, HMS *Hermes* (left) and HMS *Invincible*, which set sail from Southampton on 5 April. The fleet also included three nuclear submarines, HMS *Conqueror*, *Spartan* and *Splendid*. Before the crisis, *Hermes* had been scheduled to be decommissioned in 1982. Instead, she became the task force's flag ship, carrying Sea Harrier jump-jets and Sea King helicopters to the South Atlantic, as well as troops, including these men of 40 Commando Royal Marines (below), keeping up their fitness on the long voyage south. They bring to mind the Duke of Wellington's reputed remark about his army: 'I don't know what effect these men will have upon the enemy, but, by God, they frighten me.' The men did also get time off to relax on deck during the voyage (left). Other troops travelled on the ocean liner *Canberra*, which was requisitioned on its return to Southampton on 7 April and despatched to the South Atlantic within two days. A month later the *QE2* was also requisitioned as a troop ship and sent to the war zone.

INTO BATTLE

Personnel on HMS *Hermes* re-arming Sea King helicopters with torpedoes during the conflict (bottom left). The Sea Kings were used to locate and attack enemy submarines, as well as for shifting troops and materiel. The greatest danger faced by British ships came from the air. The Argentines flew American-made Skyhawk and French-made Mirage III fighter planes; they also had a number of Super Etendard fighters (also French-made) that could launch Exocet missiles. These destroyed HMS *Sheffield* and the supply ship MV *Atlantic Conveyor*. The blazing ship here (left) is the frigate HMS *Antelope* which exploded in San Carlos Bay on 24 May. President François Mitterrand stopped the export of Exocets from France to Argentina, along with spare parts for their planes. Mitterrand was one of two national leaders who gave unequivocal support to Britain, the other being the Chilean president, Augusto Pinochet. British troops, like the men coming ashore below, began landing in force in late May.

On the diplomatic front, the US and the EEC were stirred into action. The EEC approved trade sanctions against Argentina, and NATO and the Commonwealth countries gave Britain their backing. The Americans, much to the surprise of most Britons, were at first equivocal in their support of Britain's military response to the invasion of what Reagan called 'that little ice-cold bunch of land down there'. Wary of communists making headway in South America, their own backyard, the Americans were not rushing to undermine Galtieri and his right-wing junta. Alexander Haig, the American Secretary of State, began a round of shuttle diplomacy between Britain and Argentina, but met with obduracy on both sides. In the end, America did substantially help Britain by allowing its task force to use US facilities on Ascension Island, en route to the Falklands, and by supplying invaluable intelligence on the Argentinians' military operations.

British troops arrive

On 25 April men of the SAS and Royal Marines captured South Georgia. A very relieved Mrs Thatcher told a press conference: 'Just rejoice at that news and congratulate our forces and the marines.' A week later the first reconnaissance troops landed on the Falklands proper, while a Vulcan bomber and Harrier jump-jets rendered Port Stanley's airstrips virtually unusable to Argentine planes. The *Sun* reported these developments under the football-inspired headline: 'BRITAIN 6 (Georgia, two airstrips, three warplanes), ARGENTINA 0.'

Of all the tabloids, the *Sun* relished its nationalistic role and it would soon come up with its most infamous and shamelessly jubilant headline of the war: 'Gotcha!'. On 2 May, the British submarine HMS *Conqueror* sank the Argentine cruiser *General Belgrano*, killing 368 crewmen on board. It was one of the most controversial incidents of the entire war and the controversy only grew as it later emerged that the cruiser had been sailing away from the Falklands when it was hit and was actually outside Britain's declared 200-mile exclusion zone around the islands. The *Belgrano* incident eventually attracted much criticism, especially from the Labour MP Tam Dalyell, but at the time war still raged. Two days after the *Belgrano* was sent to the bottom, Argentinian aircraft sank HMS *Sheffield* with Exocet missiles. More than 40 crewmen were killed or maimed.

In the following weeks, frenzied diplomacy, including a peace plan proposed by the Peruvians, failed to stop the war. Meanwhile, British aircraft and warships bombarded Argentine positions in and around Port Stanley. On 21 May, British units under Major General Jeremy Moore began landing at San Carlos on East Falkland – the long-awaited land battle was about to begin. At the same time, the Argentinian air force still posed a serious threat to British shipping, and in the next few days the vessels *Ardent*, *Antelope*, *Coventry* and MV *Atlantic Conveyor* were sunk or badly hit. Despite these losses, British ground troops pressed forward and the nation was introduced to a new word, 'yomping' – Marine slang for marching

THE FLEET RETURNS
A flotilla of small vessels turns out to escort a returning Royal Navy aircraft carrier into Portsmouth harbour on 30 July, 1982, bringing victorious troops home from the Falklands War (below). A similar welcome greeted the docking of HMS *Invincible* in September, with a later contingent of returning troops (bottom right). But along with the euphoria came grief – for those who had died or been wounded. Prominent among the fallen was Lieutenant Colonel H Jones, VC, who was buried in the Falklands at the Blue Beach war cemetery in Port San Carlos, close to where he had fallen (right). There was also anger, with many deploring Mrs Thatcher's apparent enthusiasm for the campaign. Denis Healey talked about her 'glorying in the slaughter', although he later apologised for the remark. When told by a heckler in June 1983 that at least, regarding the war, the Prime Minister had had guts, Neil Kinnock retorted: 'It's a pity that other people had to leave theirs on the ground at Goose Green to prove it.'

with full kit. On 28 May members of 2 Para defeated the Argentinians at Goose Green and Darwin, taking more than a thousand prisoners. Britain now had a new hero, Lieutenant Colonel H Jones, who was posthumously awarded a VC for leading a gallant charge that brought his death.

Diplomatic efforts continued, but by this time the war's momentum was unstoppable. On 8 June Welsh Guards landing at Fitzroy near Bluff Cove were attacked by enemy aircraft with the loss of 51 men. Just three days later the British advanced on Port Stanley itself. More names entered the British public's lexicon – Tumbledown, Wireless Ridge, Mount William – as the fierce firefights continued around the hills above the tiny capital. Finally, on 14 June, the Argentinian commander General Mario Menendez realised his situation was hopeless and surrendered to Moore. Nearly 10,000 Argentine troops laid their weapons down. Moore's message to the government read: 'The Falkland Islands once more are under the government desired by their inhabitants – God save the Queen.'

The afterglow of victory

On 21 July HMS *Hermes*, the Navy's flagship, arrived back in Portsmouth to thousands of cheering spectators and a flypast by RAF Harriers. Margaret Thatcher herself was landed by helicopter onto the carrier to meet the captain and crew before the vessel docked. The scenes at Portsmouth reflected a wave of

national relief, euphoria and chauvinistic pride. But not everyone shared the jubilant mood; after all, the war had cost the lives of more than 250 members of the task force, with 300 wounded. Argentine casualties are not known precisely, but it is thought more than 650 of their troops, some of them teenage conscripts, had died. On 26 July a thanksgiving service was held in St Paul's Cathedral in London at which Robert Runcie, the Archbishop of Canterbury – himself a veteran of the Second World War – instead of striking a triumphalist note as the government wished, reminded everyone that war was a terrible thing, and 'people are mourning on both sides in this conflict'.

Thatcher herself sensed a turning point in her fortunes and was quick to capitalise on it. In early July she gave a speech in which she talked about the nation not being in retreat any more, of finding a new confidence 'born in the economic battles at home and found true 8,000 miles away ...' She then went on to declare emphatically that 'Britain found herself again in the South Atlantic and will not look back from the victory she has won'.

A SECOND VICTORY

The swift victory in the Falklands War reversed the political momentum for Margaret Thatcher and her government. Resisting the temptation to milk the patriotic fervour straightaway and hold a snap election later in 1982, Thatcher opted instead to bide her time. In fact she needed every ounce of the Falklands feel-good factor to counterbalance the gloomy economic news. During 1982 unemployment was heading towards 3 million, economic growth was negligible and industrial output was the lowest for more than 25 years. The only saving grace was that by the end of the year inflation had receded to 5 per cent.

In the early months of 1983, the Falklands bubble had still not burst. And with inflation – the Tories' main enemy of economic prosperity – still seemingly under control, Thatcher decided to hold the election on 9 June. This time she had to defeat not only Labour but the combined energies of the SDP/Liberal Alliance, who, despite suffering from the Falklands effect, had been scoring well in the polls.

On the campaign trail
Labour struggled during the run-up to the election. The very issues that had alienated many on the right of the party and spawned the SDP – especially getting

YOUTH PROTEST
Young people queue outside the Houses of Parliament on 25 February, 1982, waiting to lobby Norman Tebbit, the Conservative Employment Secretary, about the government's youth policies. Tebbit had quickly gained a reputation as a hardliner. After the riots of 1981 he was quoted as saying: 'I grew up in the 1930s with an unemployed father. He didn't riot. He got on his bike and looked for work, and he kept looking till he found it.' From then on the phrase 'on yer bike' was for evermore associated with Tebbit. Unemployment was particularly high among young people. In 1983 the government's youth policies were based around the Youth Training Scheme (YTS), aimed at school leavers of 16 and 17 years of age. Trainees were paid on the course they chose, but in doing so they forfeited their dole money and were no longer counted among the unemployed.

LET BATTLE COMMENCE
Mrs Thatcher takes a closer look at photographers during the election campaign (right). The government's strategy was to thrust her to the fore whenever possible, emphasising her leadership qualities in a not-very-subtle reminder of the recent war. In 1983 Tory strategists also made much of the in-fighting going on within Labour, producing this Punch and Judy cartoon poster of Tony Benn and Michael Foot (below). The SDP-Liberal Alliance campaigned somewhat predictably on a 'fresh start', drawing attention to Labour's left-wing extremists and the Tories' poor record on industry. Labour, meanwhile, struggled. The rhetoric of Michael Foot (left) may have come across well in parliamentary debate, but this did not transfer onto television screens. And the policies that Labour were promoting seemed to go down as badly with the public as they had with the high-profile Labour members who left the party to found the SDP. Labour MP Gerald Kaufman was moved to call his party's 1983 manifesto 'the longest suicide note in history'.

rid of Britain's nuclear deterrent and leaving the EEC – were, according to the polls, putting off potential voters. While Labour floundered, the government's campaign was professional, slick and well-funded – the Tories spent nearly £3.8 million compared to Labour's £2.56 million – but the difference was as much about organisation as money. Clive James, writing in the *Observer* about Michael Foot's campaign, noted the difference in Tory and Labour efficiency: 'To follow the unscrupulous Mrs Thatcher it was merely necessary to climb aboard the bus which had so cynically been provided, but to follow Mr Foot required acumen, maps and a current Access card.'

On 9 June the great British electorate voted Mrs Thatcher in for a second term with a huge landslide majority of 144, an increase of 101 seats from 1979. Labour won 209 seats while the Alliance had a disappointing 23. Given that the Alliance took 25.4 per cent of the vote to Labour's 27.6 per cent, David Steel had some justification for feeling 'a real sense of outrage at the vast number of votes we picked up with so little to show for it in the way of seats'.

New faces at the top

The re-elected Prime Minister lost no time in reshuffling her Cabinet, recasting it more in her own image. Francis Pym, the Foreign Secretary, was sacked and replaced with the patient Sir Geoffrey Howe. Nigel Lawson, whose intellect Thatcher

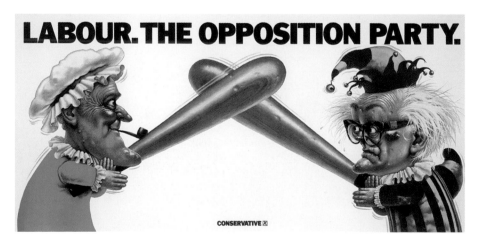

LABOUR. THE OPPOSITION PARTY.

CONSERVATIVE ☒

PINTS FOR POLITICIANS
The 1983 election was a disaster for Labour, but Neil Kinnock had a good campaign. At Bridgend on 7 June he delivered a memorably passionate speech, his voice hoarse, which warned: 'If Margaret Thatcher wins on Thursday, I warn you not to be ordinary. I warn you not to be young. I warn you not to fall ill. I warn you not to get old.' By the time this photograph was taken of Kinnock enjoying a pint with Denis Healey (on the left) and the former West German Chancellor, Willy Brandt, he had already been elected Labour Party leader, with Roy Hattersley as deputy leader. The pair, representing Labour's 'soft' left and centre right, were generally thought to have the best chance of restoring the party's electoral fortunes and were dubbed Labour's 'dream ticket'.

admired, became Chancellor; the ever-flamboyant Michael Heseltine went to the Ministry of Defence; and the clever and loyal Leon Brittan moved from the Treasury to replace Willie Whitelaw at the Home Office. Cecil Parkinson, the suave architect of the Tory election victory, became Trade and Industry Secretary, but he soon had to resign after details of his affair with his secretary, Sara Keays, were published in *The Times*.

Meanwhile, it was all-change at the top of the Labour Party. Immediately after their crushing election defeat, Foot and Denis Healey announced they were standing down as leader and deputy leader respectively, opening the way for a leadership contest in the autumn. On 2 October Neil Kinnock, perceived to be on the 'soft' left of the party, became Labour's new leader. The son of a Welsh coal miner, Kinnock had been one of the few bright spots in Labour's campaign. Over the following years he did much to face down the extremists in the party and lay the foundations of Tony Blair's New Labour project in the 1990s.

For the SDP and the Liberals, the election also brought change. The SDP leader, Roy Jenkins, held onto Hillhead, but Shirley Williams and Bill Rodgers had lost their seats, reducing the gang of four to two. The rest of the party was decimated, with their total number of MPs being reduced from 29 to 6. The party's patrician image, its lack of grass-roots' support and the Falklands factor that drew votes to Mrs Thatcher were all blamed for its demise. The Liberals fared better, increasing their seats from 11 to 17. The Alliance regrouped, with David Owen replacing Jenkins as leader of the SDP. Owen's relationship with David Steel was uneasy, but at first the two Davids rallied support for the Alliance.

TORY BIG BEASTS

Mrs Thatcher's post-election cabinet included Nigel Lawson (above) as Chancellor of the Exchequer, and Michael Heseltine (right) at Defence. Nigel Lawson had worked as a financial journalist then editor of the *Spectator* before being elected an MP in 1974. He was one of the few people whose intellect Thatcher respected. He remained Chancellor for six years, implementing many radical policies, before resigning in 1989. Heseltine, known popularly as 'Tarzan' for his flowing locks and dashing style, was renowned for his PR skills. He proved a formidable opponent of the Campaign for Nuclear Disarmament (CND) and was always a crowd-pleaser at the annual party conference. He would later challenge Thatcher for the leadership, at which point he learned the limitations of his popular appeal within his own party.

If Lawson and Heseltine brought the government continuity and credibility, Thatcher had less luck with Cecil Parkinson, one of her favourite colleagues. She had hoped to make him Foreign Secretary, but after he confided that a scandal was brewing about his affair with his former secretary Sara Keays, Thatcher decided to put him in the less high-profile post of Trade and Industry Secretary. It made no difference. On 14 October, 1983, Parkinson resigned from the government after Keays revealed she was pregnant with his child.

Setbacks and an economic upturn

Just months into Mrs Thatcher's second term, events were already throwing her government off course. In October Cecil Parkinson resigned from the Cabinet when news of an affair with his secretary was splashed all over the papers. That same month, another military storm blew up on a small island thousands of miles away. But this time, rather than taking charge at centre stage, Britain was reduced to a passive onlooker as US troops invaded the Caribbean island of Grenada, a former British colony and member of the Commonwealth.

The invasion shocked the world. The spur for it had been a military coup and the execution of the Grenadian prime minister Maurice Bishop and some of his colleagues. The coup leaders were backed by Cuba – behind whom lay the Soviet Union – and were seen as a regional threat by the USA. Despite pleas by Mrs Thatcher not to use force, President Reagan ordered the invasion to go ahead. Thatcher was humiliated, but the special relationship with America held.

At least there was better news on the economy. In December 1983 an international report declared that Britain had the fastest-growing economy in Europe. A month later a CBI survey stated that the country had the highest

continued on page 73

GOLDEN PERFORMANCE

Jayne Torvill and Christopher Dean got the nation humming Ravel's *Bolero* when they gave their classic performance to the tune at the 1984 Sarajevo winter Olympics (left). They received a standing ovation, an unprecedented maximum score of 6 for artistic interpretation from all the judges and skated off with the gold medal. It was a display full of grace and emotion by the pair from Nottingham, who already had a haul of medals from the British, European and World championships. Torvill, who worked in insurance, and policeman Dean were often linked romantically by the British press, but their chemistry remained firmly on the ice; they were always just good friends.

A NEW PRINCE

Princess Diana leaves St Mary's Hospital, London, with her newborn son Harry (soon to be christened Henry Charles Albert David Windsor) on 17 September, 1984. He was born two days previously at 4.20pm, weighing 6lb 14oz. Diana had given birth to his elder brother William in the same hospital on 21 June, 1982. Diana was already known for her natural affinity with children, and she would insist on taking a very much hands on role as a mother within the royal family.

CAPITALIST CRUSADE
The Tory policy of selling nationalised industries to private buyers accelerated during Mrs Thatcher's second and third terms. The sale of British Telecom in April 1984 (left) was deemed a huge success, and over the next few years the likes of British Aerospace, Britoil, Cable and Wireless, British Gas, British Airways and Rolls-Royce followed suit. Nigel Lawson was one of the prime architects of privatisation. Back in 1981 he had set the tone by declaring that nationalised industries should be privatised unless there was an 'overwhelming case' for not doing so. This ideal became the mainstay of the Tories' policy of 'popular capitalism'.

manufacturing orders for seven years. So 1984 started on a note of economic optimism. This would enable the Conservatives to develop the policy that became inextricably linked with the Thatcher era: privatisation.

Naturally the privatisation policy was opposed by the Opposition, but there was also great resistance among the media and the general public to what was popularly described as 'selling off the family silver'. Nevertheless, when British Telecom was put up for sale in April 1984, some 2 million Britons applied for the prospectus. On the morning of 3 December the first instalment of shares went on sale at 130 pence each; by the evening they were worth more than 170 pence each. In the end, the sale of the company raised £3 billion for government coffers, while the quick profits made by individuals kindled more enthusiasm from the public for the privatisation of other state industries in the years to come.

THE MINERS' STRIKE

There were many in the country during the 1980s who thought that Thatcher and her Conservative colleagues should be stopped, and none more so than Arthur Scargill, leader of the National Union of Mineworkers (NUM). In March 1984 he called tens of thousands of miners out on strike at the start of what became one of the most bitter industrial disputes in British history. The war of nerves between the government and the NUM lasted for a year. Night after night, the scenes of battle played out on the nation's television screens as swaying lines of policemen struggled to hold back the pickets trying to stop delivery lorries and former colleagues from entering collieries. Mining communities and even families were torn apart as they were divided into strikers and non-strikers. Violence was frequent and hardship for the striking miners and their families was widespread.

The show-down between the government and the miners was, it seems, inevitable. The Conservatives knew that at some point they would have to tackle the problem of a loss-making, overmanned industry whose workers were capable of bringing down a government. But they also knew they would be in for a fight – especially after the fiery Scargill had become NUM president following the retirement of the more moderate Joe Gormley in 1982. In 1981 Mrs Thatcher had given way before a threatened national strike over a proposal to close a number of pits. With winter approaching and coal stocks low, this was not the time to pick a fight

'This battle is certainly about more than the miners' union. It is for the right to work. It is for the right to preserve our pits. It is for the right to preserve this industry ...'

Arthur Scargill, speaking at a special national conference of miners' delegates on 19 April, 1984

with the NUM. But the Prime Minister and her cabinet were making preparations. New employment legislation introduced in 1980 and 1982 had eroded the power of the trade unions, declaring secondary picketing and the closed shop illegal, and making trade unions liable for damages in some circumstances. A system of mobile

COMRADE ARTHUR

Arthur Scargill (left), who succeeded Joe Gormley as president of the National Union of Miners, polarised opinion in Britain as much as Margaret Thatcher. He was a working-class hero to his supporters, but a dangerous extremist to the right-wing press. Born near Barnsley in Yorkshire, Scargill grew up to be a miner like his father before him. He first came to national prominence during the miners' strike in 1972, when he led a mass picket of 15,000 miners that closed the coke depot at Saltley in Birmingham. Perhaps that success contributed to his belief that he could do the same against Thatcher. In the 1984 strike he led from the front, galvanising the striking miners with his untempered oratory often shouted through a megaphone. He is seen here in typical pose as he addresses a mass rally in London held in support of the miners on 27 June, 1984.

Although the miners came under severe political and financial pressure (strikers were not allowed to receive social security payments), they were sustained by their local communities and support from the wider public. Wives and other relatives and friends threw themselves into the task of raising money and keeping the strikers' spirits up. Volunteers with collection buckets appeared outside pubs, factories and shops. Women clubbed together to set up soup kitchens, able to feed hundreds of strikers. In Stainforth, south Yorkshire, a typical close-knit mining community, the local sewing factory and supermarket arranged for money to be collected for the cause. Other groups also helped out. Trade unionists sent Christmas parcels of food and toys to families of striking miners. And the gay community formed the Lesbians and Gays Support the Miners (LGSM) organising collections, music gigs and activities such as sponsored cycle rides. They raised and donated £20,000.

police units was now set up to enforce the new law and to combat secondary 'flying pickets'. Some 26 million tons of coal were stockpiled at power stations. In some cases, helipads were installed so that crucial materials could be flown in.

In September 1983, with preparations to combat a strike in place, Thatcher appointed Ian MacGregor, the former chairman of British Steel, as head of the National Coal Board (NCB). MacGregor was a controversial figure, very much in tune with the government's pro-privatisation stance. At British Steel he had overseen plant closures and thousands of redundancies. He and Scargill faced each other from the outermost ends of the political spectrum.

The strike begins

The flashpoint was MacGregor's announcement that he wanted to close 20 uneconomic pits, with the loss of 20,000 jobs. Scargill wanted a strike in response, but was reluctant to hold a ballot, as now demanded by law, to authorise a national walk-out. There was some doubt about whether there would

'Our customers are prepared for a very lengthy strike ... they have put together large stocks because of their concern about the fairly wild statements that have been made.'

Ian MacGregor, chairman of the National Coal Board

PEACEFUL PROTEST
On 30 May, 1984, Arthur Scargill was arrested for 'obstruction' at the Orgreave coking plant near Sheffield after becoming involved in a scuffle with the police over the movement of pickets. In protest over his arrest, a group of miners occupied the NCB's headquarters in London (above). Having made their point, they vacated the premises peacefully. Scargill was charged and ordered by the court to pay a £250 fine along with £750 in costs.

be enough support to carry a stike: many politically moderate miners, particularly in the Midlands, had indicated a preference to keep working. Scargill opted to give NUM backing to local strikes where individual collieries were threatened, hoping that as these spread around the country the effect would be a national strike without the need for a vote. He also made plans to bus in thousands of flying pickets to deter would-be workers.

The dispute began in earnest on 6 March, 1984, when miners at Cortonwood colliery in Yorkshire came out in protest at the Coal Board's closure plans. Within about a week more than half of the nation's 187,000 miners had joined them and some 130 pits were idle. But a split over the lack of a ballot was evident from the start. At the Bilston Glen colliery in Scotland, scuffles broke out when pickets tried to stop miners going to work. At Harworth in Nottinghamshire working miners were helped to brave the picket lines by the support of their wives.

The NUM's decision not to hold a national ballot rankled with many miners and it was officially challenged by the leader of the Leicestershire branch of the NUM. At a meeting at the NUM's headquarters in Sheffield on 12 April the national executive decided to uphold its position, much to the delight of the hardline supporters who had gathered outside the building. But the moderates remained unhappy, and the division between miners deepened. In the long run, the lack of a national ballot would fatally damage the NUM's cause.

OUT IN FORCE

The miners' strike led to a protracted police operation. When these bobbies (left) were photographed in March 1984, in the very early stages of the strike, relations between police and miners were relatively equable. But this changed as the strike went on and the situation grew increasingly bitter, with rising levels of aggression on both sides. On 9 April, 60 pickets were arrested at Babbington colliery in Nottinghamshire after police were pelted with stones. At Cresswell pit in Derbyshire, police were taken by surprise when around a thousand flying pickets turned up to try to stop non-striking miners going to work, but the colliery was kept open. It was in the so-called Battle of Orgreave at the Orgreave coking plant in South Yorkshire – where these ranks of mounted police (right) stand ready for action on 2 June – that the atmosphere between the two sides changed dramatically.

In general, the police were far better prepared for the miners' strike of 1984 than their colleagues had been in the previous decade. And they were deployed in unprecedented numbers earning equally unprecedented sums in overtime pay. The police containing the pickets at Orgreave were drawn from the forces of no fewer than ten counties, all drafted in to make sure the coking plant was kept open. On 18 June, amid escalating violence, the mounted police made a decisive showing, charging at and dispersing groups of miners. The next day, events at Orgreave dominated Prime Minister's Questions in the House of Commons. Neil Kinnock declared that Thatcher's 'absolutism' had 'brought us Britain's first billion pound industrial dispute' and 'violent conflict on a scale that has virtually been unknown in this country'. An unrepentant Mrs Thatcher retorted that not only was the Coal Board's profitability at stake but the whole issue of law and order.

Showdown at Orgreave

In May the conflict escalated at British Steel's Orgreave coking plant near Sheffield. Scargill was determined that the convoys of coke lorries must be stopped from entering the plant and organised a huge picket of miners to gather outside the gates. There they were met by massed ranks of police, summoned from ten counties, who were charged with keeping the way open for the lorries. At nine o'clock on the morning of 29 May, the first of 34 lorries made its way to the plant's entrance and was met by a huge surge from the massed pickets. Stones, bricks and smoke bombs were hurled, and fights broke out between the miners and police armed with truncheons and riot shields. This was just the first of many such confrontations, as the stand-off at Orgreave continued throughout the first half of June. The climax came on 18 June when the

'What we have got is an attempt to substitute the rule of the mob for the rule of law, and it must not succeed.'

Margaret Thatcher

continued on page 81

THE BATTLE LOST

Cordoned off by police, striking miners watch helplessly as full trucks of coal depart for their destinations. Analysts have pointed to several factors as to why the miners lost their ultimate battle. For one thing the NUM leadership called the strike in spring, when the demand for coal was on a downward curve, so the effects of any action would take a long time to bite. Furthermore, the NUM's failure to hold a ballot – which led to the formation in Nottinghamshire of the breakaway Union of Democratic Mineworkers – not only meant that the strike lost credibility as a national cause, but also that coal was still being produced throughout the strike. But perhaps the greatest factors lay not with the NUM but with the government and police, who were prepared for this strike as never before. Mrs Thatcher was determined to curb the power that had enabled unions to hold governments to ransom in the 1970s. With full stockpiles of coal built up at power stations, a police force ready for the challenge and new legislation in place making it easier to arrest and prosecute individual miners, this was a battle the Prime Minister was determined to win. At the end of the year-long strike, the police claimed that they had deployed an extra 3,000 officers per day and had made more than 10,000 arrests. At times it was alleged that the police lost their discipline and over-reacted – Arthur Scargill and others were deeply critical of police conduct at Orgreave and South Yorkshire Police would eventually be forced to pay compensation to some miners. But the daily scenes of police contending with bricks and stones, torn-up fence posts, ball bearings and other missiles thrown at them made it harder for Labour politicians to defend the miners' actions and alienated public opinion.

showdown between thousands of pickets and the serried ranks of police exploded in the so-called Battle of Orgreave. It was a hot summer's day and the police acted with force. Mounted officers were deployed to disperse the crowd, and the fighting continued in the nearby village. The injured included Scargill himself. The NUM called off the pickets from Orgreave the very next day. In the following month the two sides in the dispute had another go at coming to an agreement, but the terms put forward by the NCB were rejected by Scargill. And so the strike dragged on.

Another major conflict arose at Maltby in South Yorkshire on 21 September. Later that month, the NUM were put on the defensive when some moderate mineworkers went to court to challenge the legality of the strike: the judge ruled that it was unlawful because a national ballot had not been held. Arthur Scargill dismissed the judgment, describing it as 'another attempt by an unelected judge to interfere in the union's affairs', but it reinforced the view of many in Britain that the striking miners were acting above the law. It also contributed, in December 1984, to the formation of the breakaway Union of Democratic Mineworkers, which deepened the split in the mining community.

More serious for the reputation and the morale of the union was an incident that took place on 30 November in South Wales. Two strikers tried to stop a taxi taking a miner to work at the Merthyr Vale pit by dropping a concrete block at the car from a bridge. The 46-pound block killed the taxi driver, David Wilkie, a father of four; his passenger was traumatised but uninjured. The loss of life shocked the nation, but it was not the only death of the strike: six pickets also died and three teenage boys who had been scavenging for coal on a slag heap.

Back to work

As 1984 came to a close, with ever-worsening hardship facing the miners and their families, the NCB lured nearly 20,000 men back to work with the promise of Christmas bonuses. During the early months of 1985 the drift back continued. When the Energy Secretary Peter Walker announced that no power cuts would be necessary during the winter, the NUM could see the writing on the wall. Realising that the best outcome now was to lose with pride intact, the men voted to return to work on 3 March, almost exactly a year after the strike had started.

Many miners marched back to the sound of the colliery band, with banners held high and tears in their eyes, but there was no hiding the enormity of the defeat. The strike destroyed the aura of the trade union movement as a whole – Norman Tebbit said that Thatcher had broken 'a spell'. The government's victory had cost the taxpayer nearly £3 billion, had damaged sterling, increased the jobless and worsened the balance of payments. For the mining industry and the mining communities it supported, it was a disaster from which they never recovered.

APPROACHING THE ENDGAME
Pickets at Tilmanstone Colliery in Kent in March 1985 as the year-long strike was drawing to a close. Kent miners were the only NUM branch to vote against the return to work. The NCB had considered closing Tilmanstone in 1967 and its days were now numbered: the colliery would close in 1986 and many more would face the same fate. The strike proved to be an unequivocal victory for the government and a huge embarrassment for the Labour Party, whose ministers instinctively sided with the miners but were forced to condemn picket violence. Neil Kinnock, himself the son of a coal miner, personally disliked Scargill and his militant methods. In the end the government did not gloat publicly in its victory. The Coal Board simply declared: 'There is no victory. The coal industry has lost, it's the victim.'

IN SEARCH OF SECURITY IN 1984

'It was a bright cold day in April, and the clocks were striking thirteen.' So begins George Orwell's great novel *1984*, first published in 1949. By the time the year 1984 actually did arrive, Orwell's nightmarish vision of a totalitarian state run by 'the Party' was almost part of the national psyche, so perhaps it was inevitable that the country's security would be very much on the agenda. The Falklands conflict in 1982 had heightened an awareness that war could arise almost out of the blue, far more easily than people had previously imagined. The Cold War remained an ominous backdrop to people's lives. There was huge tension after a Korean airliner which had strayed into Soviet air space was shot down by the Soviets in September 1983, with the loss of 269 lives.

In June 1984 the latent fears of nuclear conflict were spectacularly brought into the pop charts by Frankie Goes to Hollywood with their smash hit, 'Two Tribes'. The song opened with air-raid sirens and an official-sounding voice-over pronouncing, 'When you hear the air attack warning you and your family must take cover'. In the accompanying video actors dressed as Ronald Reagan and the Soviet Union's President Chernenko wrestled with each other.

Star wars and Greenham Common
Frankie's song also included the line 'Switch off your shield', which was probably a reference to President Reagan's Strategic Defense Initiative (SDI), which he launched in March 1983. The ambitious idea was to establish a system of linked satellites that would employ laser-beam technology to destroy incoming enemy missiles. Critics of the initiative believed that it was too futuristic, would be too expensive and would heighten Cold War tensions. It was quickly dubbed 'Star Wars' after the 1977 film by George Lucas.

Back on the terrestrial level, tensions were raised by the arrival of American missiles in Britain and in other parts of Western Europe. In the late 1970s, NATO had been alarmed at the threat posed by the Soviets' deployment of SS20 nuclear missiles and had asked the US to deploy Cruise and Pershing II missiles in Europe in response. As the date of their arrival in late 1983 drew closer, members of the Campaign for Nuclear Disarmament (CND) organised protests. On 22 October,

CAMP LIFE
Protesters outside the Greenham Common air base sit around on chairs and battered sofas while their food cooks on an open fire – even serious protest had its downtime. The peace camp formed at the air base, which was under US military control, in protest at a NATO-inspired plan to deploy nuclear missiles there. From time to time the authorities would try to clamp down on the women keeping their vigil.

At daybreak on 4 April, 1984, for example, bailiffs and some 300 police descended on the camp and arrested 30 people. The flashpoint for the eviction was a government plan to build a new access road on land adjacent to the base. A few women tried to resist arrest, but most went peacefully, prepared to return to fight another day. In fact, they did not have to wait for another day: by nightfall many had set up a number of small camps around the base's perimeter.

1983, hundreds of thousands of people across Europe joined rallies to express their abhorrence of nuclear arms. London ground to a standstill as some 200,000 people gathered in Hyde Park to hear speeches from the likes of Neil Kinnock and the Liberal MP Paddy Ashdown, while Joan Ruddock, the head of CND, told reporters that the demonstration had 'put paid to the notion that the peace movement is on its last legs'.

But the protesters could not stop the missiles reaching Greenham Common, a military airbase near Newbury in Berkshire. Their arrival, in the middle of November 1983, was greeted by a crowd of angry women who had formed a peace camp there back in 1981, in anticipation of the missiles' deployment. The camp remained a fixture of anti-nuclear protest throughout the 1980s (it eventually closed in 2000), and scenes of women of all ages, linking arms, holding candles, waving placards, sticking flowers into the wire security fences, and singing 'All we are saying, is give peace a chance', became iconic images in the media.

GCHQ and spies

Civil liberties were very much in the air, heightened by the Orwellian context. Phone-tapping had been used by various governments before the 1980s to keep tabs on suspected 'subversives': the miners' leaders Arthur Scargill and Mick McGahey, for example, were under such surveilliance both up to and during the miners' strike. In January 1984 the issue of civil liberties became a hot political potato when the government announced that members of the 7,000-strong staff at GCHQ – the military intelligence-gathering centre in Cheltenham – would have the right to belong to a trade union withdrawn from March onwards. Although the government offered a compensatory payment of £1,000 to each member of staff, there were angry protests and eventually 14 workers were sacked. GCHQ won a High Court case against the government on technical grounds, but this was overturned by a Court of Appeal. (The union ban remained in force until it was repealed by Tony Blair's government following his election win in 1997.)

Then, in April 1984, the public were reminded that intelligence gathering and spying were still crucial to the national interest when an MI5 officer named Michael Bettaney was sentenced to 23 years for spying for the Soviet Union. A year later, an East German named Reinhard Schulze – apparently an innocuous kitchen designer – and his wife Sonja, a translator, living in Cranford, Middlesex, were charged with spying. Special Branch officers found coded messages inside a can of air-freshener and false-identity documents at their home. They were later sentenced to ten years.

Those falling foul of the Official Secrets Act were not limited to individuals working for foreign governments. In 1983 a 23-year-old Foreign Office employee named Sara Tisdall leaked to the *Guardian* confidential information about the arrival of Cruise missiles in Britain. She was found out, put on trial and sentenced to six months in jail. In February 1985 another civil servant, this time an official at the Ministry of Defence named Clive Ponting, was tried for sending two classified documents about the sinking of the Argentine vessel, the *General Belgrano*, to the Labour MP Tam Dalyell, who had been questioning the government's version of the sinking. On 16 February a jury acquitted Ponting of the charges – much to his own surprise (he had made sure to take his toothbrush to court in anticipation of a jail sentence). Although found innocent, Ponting nevertheless resigned from the Civil Service and pursued a career in writing and lecturing.

THE BRIGHTON BOMB

'There were no cries for help, no sound at all, just dust, clouds of dust, followed by the occasional crunch of falling masonry from somewhere above. Otherwise silence. It was eerie.' So wrote Ronald Millar, Mrs Thatcher's speech writer, after an IRA bomb exploded in Brighton's Grand Hotel on 12 October, 1984 (left). Thatcher herself was extremely lucky to escape the blast unhurt. Only minutes before the bomb went off she had been in her hotel bathroom, which was all but destroyed as the explosion ripped apart the hotel front. She was able to leave the hotel with husband Denis (right), shaken but unharmed.

The IRA lost no time in claiming responsibility. They issued the following statement: 'Today we were unlucky, but remember, we only have to be lucky once; you will have to be lucky always. Give Ireland peace and there will be no war.' One of the bombers, Patrick Magee, was caught and sentenced to 35 years; he was let out of jail in 1999 under the terms of the Good Friday Agreement.

In the same year, 1985, the British government became concerned on grounds of security about the imminent publication of a memoir called *Spycatcher* by an ex-MI5 officer named Peter Wright. Its attempt to ban both the book and its serialisation in newspapers led to a number of court cases. This was a massive boost to the book, which was published in Australia and America – in fact, almost everywhere except Britain – and sold in large numbers to people who would never have bought it without all the publicity. Eventually, having been made a laughing stock and faced with a fait accompli, the government dropped its objections.

Murder, mayhem and agreement

Two other incidents in 1984 served to illustrate the challenges faced by Britain's security services and police: the siege of the Libyan embassy and the Brighton bomb, when the IRA came close to assassinating Mrs Thatcher and her entire Conservative cabinet. In April, a small demonstration by dissident Libyans outside their country's embassy in St James's Square in London was patrolled by a handful of police officers. Suddenly shots were fired, presumed to be from inside the embassy, and WPC Yvonne Fletcher was killed. Ten others were wounded. Armed police immediately surrounded the building and a stand-off with the Libyans inside ensued. After ten days, the 30 staff were allowed to walk out and were deported. Britain broke off diplomatic relations with Libya.

The IRA, meanwhile, had been maintaining their campaign of violence both in Northern Ireland and on the mainland. On 20 July, 1982, for example, a nail-bomb went off in Hyde Park, claiming the lives of four soldiers of the Household Cavalry (and seven horses). That same day another explosive device went off at the bandstand in Regent's Park, where the Royal Green Jackets had been entertaining a summer crowd with music from *Oliver*. Fifty people were injured and six members of the band were killed.

Then, on 12 October, 1984, the IRA nearly pulled off the most spectacular of massacres when they exploded a 100-pound bomb at Brighton's Grand Hotel, where members of the government were staying for the Conservative Party conference. The blast came in the early hours of the morning and blew apart the hotel's front. The explosion killed five people and injured 34, including Norman Tebbit who had to be dug out of the rubble. He would be left with a limp, but his wife suffered far worse injuries and was paralysed for life. Those who died included the MP Sir Anthony Berry. It was nothing short of a miracle that the carnage was not far worse.

The Prime Minister, shaken but not physically hurt, insisted that the final day of the conference should go ahead as planned: anything else would be seen as a victory for the IRA. In an emotional speech, she declared that 'the fact that we are gathered here now, shocked but composed and determined, is a sign not only that this attack has failed but that all attempts to destroy democracy by terrorism will fail.' The words were brave, and her personal ratings soared, but some believe that she never quite had the same confidence after the incident.

The search for a solution

In 1985 the government took a step towards finding a peaceful solution to the sectarian violence when, on 15 November, Mrs Thatcher and the Irish Taoiseach (prime minister) Dr Garret Fitzgerald signed the Anglo-Irish Hillsborough agreement. This guaranteed that Northern Ireland would stay in the United Kingdom for as long as the majority desired it, but it also stated that ministers from Britain and the Irish Republic would meet on a regular basis to discuss security and other issues affecting the province. The 15 Unionist MPs resigned in protest at the Republic being given a say in the affairs of Northern Ireland. But the House of Commons voted overwhelmingly in favour of the agreement. More violence and political turmoil lay ahead, but Hillsborough was an important step in the Northern Ireland peace process.

LOYALIST ANGER

A Unionist crowd up to 100,000 strong gathered in Belfast on 23 November, 1985, to protest at the Anglo-Irish Agreement, signed a week earlier (left). The British and Irish governments had agreed to consider a change in the status of Northern Ireland only if a majority of the citizens of the province wanted it, but they also agreed that the Irish government be given an advisory role in areas of mutual concern, such as cross-border cooperation, security and various legal matters. The very fact that the agreement acknowledged that politicians of the Republic could have a voice in the North's affairs was anathema to Unionists, and they began a campaign to have the agreement rescinded. Many nationalists welcomed the agreement as a step towards cooperation and the eventual unification of Ireland, but Sinn Féin rejected it because it confirmed Northern Ireland as part of the UK. The agreement therefore stirred up loyalist opposition while doing little to stop IRA violence. In retrospect, it is seen as an important stepping stone on the way to the more far-reaching Belfast or Good Friday agreement, signed on 10 April, 1998.

HIGH TIDE OF THATCHERISM

By the mid-1980s Mrs Thatcher's second administration was in full swing. These were the years when the attitudes and policies later most associated with her decade in power came to the fore, as the government pushed on with radical reform in local government, higher education, the NHS, and other national institutions. Privatisation continued apace, with the sale of British Gas and British Airways. Meanwhile, the 'Big Bang' revolutionised the practices and technology of the London Stock Exchange.

RIOT SQUAD In a scene almost commonplace in the 1980s, police gird themselves for trouble, this time at the Broadwater Farm Estate, Tottenham, London, in the early hours of 6 October, 1985. Rioting began after a black woman died following a police search of her home.

THE REVOLUTION CONTINUES

This was the era when city bankers oozed the ambition of Gordon Gekko, the corrupt corporate raider in Oliver Stone's 1987 film *Wall Street*, who famously pronounced that 'greed is good' and 'lunch is for wimps'. In England – and it was particularly in southeast England – this manifested itself in the 'Loadsamoney' culture satirised by the comedian Harry Enfield. It conjures images of braces-wearing, slick-haired yuppies, armed with the great yuppy accessory – a brick-sized mobile phone. Rapid technological change had begun.

Rearranging the cabinet

Mrs Thatcher started 1985 buoyed by an upturn in the economy, by the success of the British Telecom privatisation and by clear signs that the miners' strike was beginning to peter out. She herself suffered a personal snub when her old alma mater, Oxford University, voted not to award her an honorary degree – a customary honour for prime ministers educated at Oxford – in protest against her government's education cuts.

There were some even in her own party who protested at her policies. Despite the glimmers of optimism on the economic front, the government was struggling to reduce unemployment and in the spring of 1985 Mrs Thatcher received a shot across the bows when Francis Pym, a former Foreign Secretary and leading 'Wet',

DOUBLE FIRST
Margaret Thatcher was not the only woman in the 1980s to storm a traditional male bastion. Another was the diminutive Susan Brown (right), who on 27 March, 1981, became the first woman to take part in the Oxford-Cambridge boat race. She is shown here during the weigh-in at Putney, shortly before taking her place in the boat as cox and steering Oxford to victory. In 1989 both university eights were coxed by women.

Thatcher appointed her ideological ally Norman Tebbit (below) as Conservative Party chairman in autumn 1985. For many, Tebbit epitomised the Thatcherite Tory: self-made – he left school at 16 and worked as a pilot for BOAC before becoming an MP in 1970 – plain-speaking, impatient with red tape and a great believer in self-enterprise. The Brighton bomb had left him with a permanent limp and may have diminished his vigour; but he was still a formidable operator with a sharp line in acerbic wit.

formed a dissident group called Conservative Centre Forward arguing against the government's hardline economic policies. Pym's group never posed a serious threat to Thatcher's authority, but it may have precipitated her cabinet reshuffle that September in an attempt to freshen up the government's presentation. Douglas Hurd became Home Secretary, ousting Leon Brittan, who was demoted to Trade and Industry. Norman Tebbit was made Party Chairman, while the millionaire novelist Jeffrey Archer became his deputy.

A case of déjà vu

Douglas Hurd was swiftly put to the test when, on 28 September, 1985, rioting broke out once more in Brixton. Local people, exasperated by police tactics in the area – just as they had been in 1981 – gathered ominously outside the local police station after police had accidentally shot a black woman in the course of investigating a robbery. By nightfall the mood had become ugly and groups of mainly black youths confronted riot police. Cars were set alight and shops looted as Brixton witnessed the same violent scenes as had occurred four years earlier. This time round one person died, 50 were injured and the police made more than 200 arrests.

As in 1981, the riots spread to other areas of London and elsewhere. In early October crowds started rioting in Toxteth in Liverpool after the arrest of four black youths in conjunction with a stabbing incident. In Peckham, south London, rioters set fire to a carpet warehouse. Then, in the middle of the month, some 500 policemen struggled to contain rioting at the Broadwater Farm housing estate in Tottenham, north London (see page 96). The violence claimed the life of PC Keith Blakelock. Bernie Grant, the Labour council leader in Tottenham, was widely reported to have said, 'What the police got was a bloody good hiding' – a phrase he claimed

'This is not England. This is just madness. My men are being used as target practice.'

A senior police officer, speaking after the Broadwater Farm Estate riots

CABINET FALL-OUT

Michael Heseltine leaving his London home soon after resigning as Defence Secretary over the Westland helicopters' affair. Although Heseltine was thenceforth built up in the media as an inveterate opponent and rival to Mrs Thatcher, he later put it on record that he had enjoyed a positive relationship with her until he resigned. She had appointed him to two of the biggest government departments, Environment and Defence, and 'backed my judgment on virtually every issue, putting me in the front line with two of the major issues of the first half of the 1980s: the sale of council houses and the battle with CND'. Heseltine was never entirely accepted by the old patrician Tories (Willie Whitelaw observed that he was the type of person who 'combed his hair in public'), but he was sufficiently popular with the Tory party at large to mount a serious bid for the leadership in 1990, after Thatcher's resignation. He lost out to John Major.

was taken out of context and that he was simply trying to explain the feelings of people on the estate. What he actually said was 'The youths around here believe the police were to blame for what happened on Sunday and what they got was a bloody good hiding.' The riots soon abated. But it was a salutary reminder to the government of the volatile nature of deprived urban districts in Thatcher's Britain.

Heseltine and helicopters

If Mrs Thatcher had thought her autumn cabinet reshuffle would bring some internal stability to her government, she was soon given a rude awakening at the start of 1986. She had always been wary of Michael Heseltine, her ambitious, able and flamboyant Minister of Defence; and when the cabinet debated a rescue package for an ailing British helicopter company named Westland, a row broke out between her and Heseltine that ended with the latter storming out of the discussion. The Westland affair led to the resignation not just of Heseltine but also Leon Brittan and nearly brought down the government.

Heseltine had wanted Westland to merge with a European consortium, which included British Aerospace, while the Westland directors, backed by Thatcher and Brittan, favoured purchase by the American-led Sikorsky-Fiat group. Beneath the apparent arguments were under-currents of Heseltine's pro-European views versus Thatcher's loyalty to America; another issue at stake was cabinet democracy.

BURNT-OUT IN BROADWATER

A resident of Tottenham in north London holds tight to his little girl's hand as they walk past burnt-out cars and houses on 7 October, 1985, the day after the riots there. The second spate of riots to hit British cities in the decade eerily echoed those of 1981 with their mix of racial tension, disaffected youth and heavy-handed policing. On the Broadwater Farm Estate trouble started after the police raided the home of a young black man, allegedly looking for stolen goods. During the police raid his 49-year-old mother, Cynthia Jarrett, collapsed and died of heart failure. Local outrage at her death – which came just one week after police had shot Cherry Groce in similar circumstances in Brixton – turned to riots the next day, 6 October. During the disturbance, PC Keith Blakelock was hacked to death with a machete and another policeman, PC Richard Coombes, was badly injured. In the aftermath, Winston Silcott, Engin Raghip and Mark Braithwaite were charged with Blakelock's murder, found guilty and sentenced to life imprisonment. Four years later an appeal court overturned the convictions because of doubts cast on police evidence.

ENGINE TROUBLE
Rolls-Royce, one of Britain's most iconic brand names, was sold off to private investors by the government in 1987. In fact it had been a Tory government, under Edward Heath, that in 1971 had nationalised Rolls-Royce in the first place to rescue the company from receivership. In 1973 the car division was sold off to Vickers, but the main company remained a nationalised concern, specialising in marine and aircraft engines. These two Rolls-Royce employees were photographed working on the latest version of the 535 aircraft engine in February 1985 (left).

In general, apart from the unions and Labour supporters, the government's privatisation schemes were popular, with thousands of private investors cashing in on quick rises in recently privatised share values. The former Conservative prime minister Harold Macmillan cast a brief shadow on the privatisation party when, in November 1985, he expressed his underlying disquiet at a policy of 'selling off the family silver'. For some, the idea that valuable and venerable assets were being sold by the government for instant revenue replaced, for a while, the idea that ailing, unprofitable and overmanned industries were being positively renovated. But most were happy to reap the profits. For Thatcher, the policy made political sense on several levels: it was not only good for boosting Treasury funds and extending popular capitalism, it was also, in her words, 'eroding the corrosive and corrupting effects of socialism'.

When, on 9 January, the Prime Minister told Heseltine at a cabinet meeting that his future statements on Westland would have to be cleared by the cabinet office, he resigned on the spot and marched out of No.10. He later issued a statement putting his resignation down to lack of trust: 'If the basis of trust between the Prime Minister and her Defence Secretary no longer exists, there is no place for me with honour in such a cabinet.'

The damage to the government did not end there. A letter from the Solicitor General criticising Heseltine was leaked to the press from Leon Brittan's Trade and Industry office. This was a serious breach of legal etiquette and led to fevered speculation as to who had authorised the leak. For a while even Thatcher's position seemed vulnerable as she continued to deny any involvement. The buck eventually stopped with Brittan, who resigned on 24 January. Thatcher had escaped, but the affair drew attention to her authoritarian style of leadership, which would become an increasingly significant issue as the decade wore on.

The GLC – RIP

Ministerial setbacks notwithstanding, the Thatcher revolution in mid-decade was concentrating its energies on reform. One of its most high-profile targets was the metropolitan county councils, which the government was set on disbanding. The official reason for doing away with a whole level of local government was to increase efficiency and cut red tape, but because these councils were dominated by Labour, the move was also seen as dealing a blow to the opposition at local level.

The most high-profile council to go was the Greater London Council (GLC). Led by the maverick but hugely popular Ken Livingstone – the 'Red Ken' of the tabloids – the GLC had its headquarters at County Hall, opposite the Houses of Parliament. Livingstone had made it a left-wing citadel and arranged for the ever-increasing numbers of the unemployed to be printed on a banner that was hung across its facade. On its final day of existence – 31 March, 1986 – the GLC went out literally with a bang, not a whimper, holding a huge open-air party and letting off £250,000-worth of fireworks.

THE BIG BANG AND PRIVATISATION

Another revolution took place in the world of finance, most spectacularly with the so-called Big Bang on 27 October, 1986, when many of the age-old and restrictive practices of the London Stock Exchange (LSE) were radically reformed. This resulted in the abolition of cartels; the end of the distinction between stockbrokers and jobbers (stock-exchange operators who dealt only with brokers); various mergers between UK and foreign securities firms and banks, bringing new wealth and a new international outlook to the LSE; and the computerisation of dealing systems – the frantic hand-waving hustle and bustle of brokers on the exchange floor was now replaced by a silent world of flickering VDU screens. The City

EIGHTIES ENTREPRENEURS
Alan Sugar (left) and Anita Roddick (bottom left) were two of the most high-profile business entrepreneurs to flourish in the Thatcher years. Alan Sugar came from the East End of London and showed business skills from an early age, selling car aerials from the back of his car. He founded the electronics company Amstrad in 1968, making car radios and hi-fis and, later, home computers. In 1980 the company was successfully floated on the Stock Exchange and during the decade it became a household name. The popular Amstrad PCW was launched in 1985 – principally a word processor that ran LocoScript and included a printer in the package.

Anita Roddick, shown here checking barrels of herb body shampoo, was the founder of The Body Shop, which had opened its first store in Brighton in 1976. With her mop of frizzy hair and Mediterranean looks (she had Italian ancestry), she brought a breath of pure fresh air into the pin-striped corporate culture of the Eighties. In 1984 her company, valued at £8 million, was floated on the London Stock Exchange and its shares immediately rose in price by 500 per cent. The Body Shop grew to have more than 2,000 branches in 55 countries. It was bought out by L'Oréal in 2006 for a figure in excess of £650 million.

itself to some extent lost its whiff of the gentleman's club and old-boy network, but it acquired instead a new aura as a place of ruthless whizz-kids, working hard and playing hard – and making Monopoly-sized piles of money.

The Big Bang was another significant step in the evolution of the nation's financial practices that had been started back in 1979 by Geoffrey Howe when he abolished exchange controls. With the current Chancellor, Nigel Lawson, leading the way, the government now presided over a culture of financial deregulation. Building societies were allowed to act like banks, and even, as in the case of the Abbey National, to become banks. The stipulations on mortgage lending eased to the point of recklessness and an orgy of money-borrowing produced a sharp rise in house prices and a spending boom. In a couple of years time, the boom would create inflation, the Tories' dreaded foe, but for the moment it gave many in Britain a sense of increasing affluence not felt since the 1960s.

Meanwhile, the government's privatisation crusade continued. In December 1986 it was the turn of British Gas to be offered to private shareholders. The government softened up the public with commercials broadcasting the message to

VIRGIN SANDS
Richard Branson swaps his hippy 1970s image for a business suit in this promotional photo taken in 1986. The face of the millionaire entrepreneur became instantly recognisable from his PR stunts, but behind the flamboyant exterior lurked the sharpest of business acumens. His Virgin group of companies, which had begun as a record label in 1973, multiplied over the years to include Virgin Airways in 1984 and Virgin Holidays in 1985. Branson also caught the headlines by attempting the fastest crossing of the Atlantic by boat (successfully achieved in 1986) and then traversing the same ocean by hot air balloon in 1987.

'Tell Sid', encouraging the man on the street to pass on the good news about the sale of shares by word of mouth. Whether it was the promotion or a previous experience of achieving a quick profit with British Telecom shares, the sale of British Gas went down well with the public and the offer was massively oversubscribed with about 4.5 million people buying shares.

The success was repeated with British Airways, the 'World's Favourite Airline', as its adverts proclaimed. Under Sir John King, the company had become a profitable enterprise in the early part of the Eighties and was ripe for privatisation. When this took place, in February 1987, the price of shares leaped by more than 80 per cent on the opening day of trading. In the same year Rolls-Royce and the British Airport Authority were sold off. In 1988 it was the turn of British Steel.

After a certain amount of outrage at the 'family silver' being sold had abated, privatisation caught the mood of the country. Millions of ordinary Britons who had never before owned shares plunged into the previously untraversed financial jungles, perhaps helped, as Labour claimed, by the Tories underpricing the shares to encourage sales for their own political agenda. By the end of 1990, forty

previously nationalised industries had become private companies, taking more than half a million employees into the private sector. In the final analysis, however, Mrs Thatcher's dream of creating a share-owning population never materialised. Many people declined the invitation to enter into this particular world of popular capitalism, while the majority of those who did buy shares in the privatisation boom preferred to sell them as soon as an increase in their value had made it irresistible, obviating any aim of maintaining broad-based ownership.

ALTERNATIVE VIEWS

One of the phrases most associated with Margaret Thatcher was 'There is no alternative', often shortened to the acronym TINA. The phrase was used by her and her followers to affirm confidence in the economic policies being pursued and it became a stick with which to beat both the opposition and Tory 'wets' alike. The phrase struck home with the public, too, because until the mid-Eighties the Tories enjoyed an extraordinarily easy ride from the opposition parties in Parliament. The fire and initial enthusiasm had gone out of the SDP-Liberal Alliance after the poor showing of the SDP at the 1983 general election. Labour, meanwhile, had imploded into disarray, weakened by ineffective leadership and fragmented by splits between the left and right wings of the party.

Kinnock takes on Militant
The first signs that Labour was coming to its senses and was prepared to put its house in order came at the party conference in Bournemouth in 1985. There, on

IN HARMONY
Neil Kinnock had plenty to sing about when this photograph of him was taken at the 1985 Labour Party conference (top left), with Jim Mortimer on his left and Larry Whitty on his right. He had just successfully confronted Militant Tendency in his key-note speech as party leader. Comparing Militant members to 'latter-day public schoolboys', he declared: 'It seems it matters not whether you won or lost, but how you played the game. We cannot take that inspiration from Rudyard Kipling'.

DID HATTON WRITE "ANIMAL FARM" (IT DROPPED US IN IT)

HATTON THE GOBFATHER

MILITANT TAKE NOTE
On 25 October, 1985, people in Liverpool took to the streets to express their anger at Derek Hatton and the way he was running Liverpool City Council. A few weeks earlier, at the Labour Party conference, Hatton had shouted 'liar' at Neil Kinnock speaking from the platform, while left-winger Eric Heffer marched out in protest at Kinnock's anti-Militant line. But the people of Liverpool left no doubt where their priorities lay: they wanted a working council providing services, not a left-wing political crusade.

1 October, Neil Kinnock delivered a direct and passionate attack on the Militant Tendency – a far-left Trotskyist group that had infiltrated Labour – in a speech that was later hailed as his finest hour as Labour leader. Some believe it was the turning point in Labour's fortunes and the first building block in the edifice that was to become Tony Blair's New Labour in the 1990s.

Militant activists targeted Labour councils all over the country – it had some 5,000 members nationwide – but it was in Liverpool that their power was most visible. Driven forward by deputy council leader Derek Hatton, Liverpool City Council sought confrontation with central government. It demonstrated its defiance by setting a huge council budget far in excess of government targets, risking bankrupting the city, then showed its ruthlessness by handing out redundancy notices to the council's entire staff.

RIGHT-ON ROCK

Red Wedge, a collective of rock bands (supported by comedians such as Lenny Henry, Ben Elton and Phil Jupitus), was founded in November 1985 principally by musicians Paul Weller and Billy Bragg (right). Weller is seen here (left) on stage in the final Jam gig in 1982. With their upbeat slogan, 'Move On Up! A Socialist Vision of the Future', Red Wedge aimed to reach out to young Labour voters who might otherwise have remained politically apathetic. They played at festivals, including Glastonbury, as well as at smaller venues. Apart from Weller's Style Council and Bragg, the principal band associated with Red Wedge was the Communards, while guest groups included the Blow Monkeys, Madness and the Smiths. Before the 1987 election on 12 June, Red Wedge went on a short tour to raise socialist consciousness, targeting marginal constituencies in particular. Their efforts had some effect – the percentage of young people aged between 18 and 24 who voted Labour in 1987 was considerably higher than in 1983. But Mrs Thatcher and the Tories still triumphed. Red Wedge survived for a few years but its impetus had gone and it finally folded in 1990.

Kinnock knew he had to stop Militant driving voters away from Labour. So at Bournemouth, half way through his keynote address, he went on the attack. He told the conference that Labour would never gain the confidence of a sceptical public with impossible promises, and he used Liverpool as an example: 'I'll tell you what happens with impossible promises. You start with far-fetched resolutions. They are then pickled into a rigid dogma, a code, and you go through the years sticking to that, outdated, misplaced, irrelevant to the real needs, and you end in the grotesque chaos of a Labour council – a Labour council – hiring taxis to scuttle round a city handing out redundancy notices to its own workers.'

Roy Hattersley said afterwards that the speech had changed British politics. The BBC's political editor John Cole told viewers that the Labour Party would never be the same again. Later, Peter Jay, the economist and broadcaster, said 'it was a definitive moment in the history of the party'. And Kinnock lost no time in putting his rhetoric into action: that November, after a seven-hour meeting of the Labour executive, the Liverpool district Labour Party was suspended. The following June Derek Hatton was expelled from the Labour Party. From this point on, the Labour leadership was always on the front foot in dealing with its own hardliners. Although it would take until 1997 for the public to put Labour back into power, the process of making Labour electable started in earnest in 1985.

Other voices

With the official Opposition landing more significant punches on each other than on the government, it seemed it was left to others to give voice to the widespread popular anger felt at Thatcherite policies. On the music scene, Billy Bragg, Paul

Weller and other socialist-leaning musicians formed a collective called Red Wedge in 1985 to raise young people's awareness of Labour policies with the aim – ultimately unsuccessful – of winning the 1987 election.

Protesting voices could be heard in plenty on the alternative comedy scene, a new phenomenon in entertainment that emerged in the decade and proved itself to be long-lived. Alternative comedians were young, brash, edgy and politically savvy in a way very different to mainstream British comics such as Morecambe and Wise, Benny Hill, Ronnie Barker, Ronnie Corbett and Tommy Cooper.

One of the main breeding grounds for alternative comedians was the London Comedy Store, a club that opened in Soho in 1979 and later moved to Leicester Square. Stand-up performers there included Alexei Sayle, Rik Mayall and Ade Edmondson, as well as Dawn French and Jennifer Saunders. Some of them went on to establish themselves at another club, the Comic Strip, founded in Soho by Peter Richardson. It was not long before the BBC and Channel 4 – which had become something of a haven for alternative, minority-interest programmes – came knocking on the Comic Strip's door, keen to exploit its fresh young talent.

In November 1982, BBC2 first broadcast *The Young Ones*, featuring a foursome of young, male, semi-dysfunctional student housemates – alias Mayall, Edmondson, Nigel Planer and Christopher Ryan – with Sayle as the landlord. In the same month Channel 4 put on 'Five Go Mad in Dorset', the first of a series of short films under the title *The Comic Strip Presents*. And so alternative comedy made the leap from the cosy atmosphere of small clubs into the living rooms of hundreds of thousands of television viewers, generally delighting the young and outraging the old with its iconoclastic, risqué humour.

The television showcase for alternative stand-up was *Saturday Live* (which later became *Friday Night Live*), broadcast on Channel 4 between 1985 and 1988. It also gave airtime to bands such as Eurythmics and Curiosity Killed the Cat. *Saturday Live* brought to fame Ben Elton, the spangly-suited socialist comic who specialised in ranting monologues about the iniquities of Margaret Thatcher – or 'Thatch' as he called her – and her politics. Detested by Middle-England Tories, Elton provided a genuine voice of protest and anger that opposition politicians were seldom able to match. Other stars born on the show included Julian Clary, Paul Merton and Jo Brand. Perhaps most memorable was Harry Enfield's Loadsamoney character, a plasterer made rich by the Lawson boom who flaunted his 'wad' of money at the audience. Enfield intended the character as a critical satire on the new rich of Thatcher's Britain, but the cry of 'Loadsamoney' was taken up with gusto by admiring imitators in pubs up and down the land.

GONE JUST LIKE THAT
Tommy Cooper, the 'hopeless magician', bowed out forever during a televised variety performance on 15 April, 1984. He suffered a massive heart attack on stage and was rushed to hospital, but was pronounced dead on arrival. He is seen here in his garden in 1983, with his wife Gwen wearing his trademark fez. Cooper was born in Wales in 1921 and practised magic as a boy. He honed his act during service in the Second World War, afterwards graduating to the small screen. He became a regular on Thames Television in the 1970s, winning over the nation with his bungled tricks, his catchphrases – most famously 'Just like that!' – and infectious laugh. His death came just six weeks before that of Eric Morecambe, who also died of a heart attack in a theatre. The loss of Tommy and Eric seemed a symbolic changing of the comedy order, with the old guard being replaced by the alternative comedy generation.

IT'S ALL BANANAS

Private Eye magazine remained the scourge of the establishment in the Eighties, just as it had been in the Sixties and Seventies. In 1986 Richard Ingrams, seen here standing in the magazine's office, handed over the editorship to Ian Hislop, who is holding a giant inflatable banana. This curious prop alludes to the 'Bananaballs' appeal which Hislop launched to raise money to pay for damages awarded to Sonia Sutcliffe, wife of Peter Sutcliffe, the Yorkshire Ripper. The magazine had alleged Sonia had profited from her husband's notoriety by selling her story to the newspapers. She sued *Private Eye* and on 24 May, 1989, was awarded £600,000 in damages. Outside the High Court on the Strand, Hislop declared: 'If that is justice, I'm a banana.' Claiming that the damages could close down the magazine, Hislop set up the Bananaballs fund, seeking contributions from readers. At the same time the *Eye* appealed and Sutcliffe's damages were eventually reduced to £60,000. The *Eye* donated the excess funds they received to the families of Peter Sutcliffe's victims.

Puppets and Private Eye

Other outlets for political protest – and not just against the government – were the television programme *Spitting Image* and the satirical magazine *Private Eye*. *Spitting Image*, which featured large rubber puppets, designed by Peter Fluck and Roger Law, caricatured politicians and other public figures. It was essentially a sketch show involving some of Britain's best impressionists, including Rory Bremner and John Sessions. After a slow start, it grew in popularity as it managed to make politicians both more detestable and more lovable. Geoffrey Howe was depicted as a faint-hearted nincompoop, talking to sheep; Douglas Hurd had hair like a Mr Whippy ice cream; Norman Tebbit appeared as a skinhead; Neil Kinnock was a garrulous 'Welsh windbag'; and rather cruelly Roy Hattersley was

continued on page 112

COMIC RELIEF

The Eighties was the decade when alternative comedy – edgy, abrasive, satirical and often crude – moved into the mainstream, thumbing its nose at cosy sit-coms and traditional stand-up. Indebted to a satirical tradition that went back to 'Beyond the Fringe' and 'That Was The Week That Was' in the 1960s, as well as to the surrealist world of Monty Python, alternative comedians came in many shapes and sizes. What they had in common was a manic energy and a delight in ruffling feathers.

NEW FACES OF COMEDY
The first show to bring alternative comedy to Britain's television screens was *Not the Nine O'Clock News*, a satirical current-affairs sketch show that began on BBC with a pilot series in 1979 and almost sank without trace. It was the second series, broadcast in 1980 and starring the team above – clockwise from left: Rowan Atkinson, Mel Smith, Griff Rhys Jones and Pamela Stephenson – that hit the button, winning a dedicated audience and picking up an award at the Montreux Festival. *Spitting Image* (right) first went out on ITV in 1984, bringing an entirely new meaning to the term 'puppet show'. In 1985 it, too, collected a Montreux rose. The script pulled no punches as the show became the hardest-hitting political satire on TV. Four of the impressionists are seen here beside their life-size puppets – Robin Day with trademark bow tie (Chris Barrie); Prince Philip (Jon Glover); Vincent Price (Enn Reitel); and Margaret Thatcher (Steve Nallon).

'Alternative comedy in those days had some real targets because we'd had a long period of Margaret Thatcher.'

Janet Street-Porter

COMEDY ASSORTMENT
A number of comedians launched or consolidated their careers in the 1980s, among them Billy Connolly (above) who had first come to national fame in the previous decade, helped along the way by an appearance on *Parkinson* in 1975. By the early 1980s he was already something of a national treasure and a regular in *The Secret Policeman's Ball*, alongside the likes of John Cleese. He also made a guest appearance on *Not the Nine O'Clock News* in a spoof interview conducted by

Pamela Stephenson, his future wife, impersonating Janet Street-Porter.

Lenny Henry (near right, top) broke new ground as a black comedian in Britain, coming to fame by a route that took in the working men's club circuit, the *New Faces* talent show and *Tiswas*. Henry made the jump to the alternative comedy scene in the early 1980s, bringing to life such memorable characters as Trevor MacDoughnut (inspired by newsreader Trevor McDonald), DJ Delbert Wilkins and Theophilus P Wilderbeest.

Alexei Sayle (far right, top) came from a Jewish-Liverpudlian background. He delivered loud, caustic, politically aware stand-up comedy, and also slotted into eccentric roles in sketches and comedy dramas, such as the dreaded landlord Mr Balowski in *The Young Ones*.

Ben Elton (bottom right) revelled in quick-fire political rants that became a regular part of *Saturday Live*. He also proved himself to be a talented writer, contributing to such series as *The Young Ones* and the 1980s comedy classic

Blackadder starring Rowan Atkinson, Tony Robinson and eventually a host of new comic talent including Hugh Laurie and Stephen Fry. Elton finally got his own show, *The Man from Auntie*, in 1990.

Dawn French and Jennifer Saunders (far right) had worked together since college days and honed their double act with *The Comic Strip*. Their sketch show on the BBC was launched in March 1987 and proved so popular they were still raising laughs 20 years later, despite having gone separate ways.

alway depicted spitting out huge quantities of saliva as he spoke. But beyond any doubt, the star of the show was Margaret Thatcher, a wild, macho, cigar-smoking autocrat, dressed in men's clothing and treating her colleagues as wimps.

Political satire also appeared fortnightly in *Private Eye*, the anti-establishment magazine founded in 1961. During the Thatcher era, the magazine ran its famous 'Dear Bill' column – spoof letters from Mrs Thatcher's husband Denis to a golf-playing Tory friend of his called Bill (supposedly based on the journalist Bill Deedes). There was also a regular comic strip called 'The Battle for Britain by Monty Stubble', which took off the style of boys' war comics of the 1960s and 1970s. Created by Ian Hislop and Nick Newman, it depicted a valiant band of British soldiers led by Corporal 'Taffy' Kinnock attempting to defeat the Fascist Führer, Herr Thatchler, and her underlings, including von Tebbit, Rudolph Hesseltine and Lord Howe-Howe. The series, which ran from 1983 to 1987, captured the prevailing view of a disorganised, fractious Labour Party gallantly failing to overcome the autocratically led Conservatives.

SPORTING HIGHS AND LOWS

For British sports fans, the Eighties were mostly a disappointment with a few notable exceptions – moments of glory that lit up the nation and quickly became treasured memories. Ian Botham's magnificent Ashes-winning knocks against Australia in 1981, for example, provided cricket with one such moment of glory. In stark contrast, three years later England suffered a whitewash – the first in its history – in the 1984 test series against a hugely talented West Indies side fielding the likes of Viv Richards and Gordon Greenidge among their batsman, with Malcolm Marshall and Michael Holding leading the fearsome bowling attack.

On the rugby field, the Welsh dominance of the 1970s was over. England won the grand slam in the 1980 Five Nations Championship, with a team captained by Bill Beaumont which also included England's future world-cup winning manager, Clive Woodward. Scotland won the championship once in the decade and Ireland twice, but France were the in-form side, winning no fewer than six times – although they were forced to share the honours on three occasions, once each with Ireland, Scotland and Wales.

Year of the underdog

In athletics a constant sense of underachievement during the decade was partly assuaged by the gold-winning Olympic performances of Sebastian Coe, Steve Ovett, Daley Thompson and Tessa Sanderson in 1980 and 1984. Sanderson surprised even herself when she took gold in the javelin in Los Angeles, the first black British athlete to win an Olympic gold medal.

One of the biggest surprises of the 1985 sporting year came in snooker, when the Northern Irish player Dennis Taylor won the world championship for the first

THE LONDON MARATHON – THE START OF SOMETHING BIG

The London Marathon, one of the annual highlights of Britain's sporting calendar today, started life in the Eighties. The massed ranks of runners shown here (left) are setting off in the 1986 race, one beset by strong winds and rain. The very first London Marathon took place five years earlier, on 29 March, 1981, when a total of 7,747 competitors set off from Blackheath hoping to make it to the finishing line on Constitution Hill. Some 1,500 runners succumbed to exhaustion, but the vast majority made it. Winners in the men's event were the Norwegian Inge Simonsen and the American Dick Beardsley, who crossed the line together holding hands. The women's event was won by a British runner, Joyce Smith. The same year saw the launch of another iconic race in June: the Great North Run, a half-marathon course from Newcastle upon Tyne to South Shields, which is now the biggest race in the country, attracting more than 50,000 runners in 2008. Through races like these, long-distance running ceased to be the preserve of an elite few, as thousands of amateur runners proved they could do it too: more than three-quarters of a million people have completed the London Marathon since it began and a wheelchair marathon was added in 1983. The main race is particularly noted for attracting runners prepared to don fancy-dress costumes to raise money for charity, making it one of the biggest annual fund-raising events in the world. This human caterpillar (below) was taking part in 1986.

ON CUE
Snooker came of age in the Eighties, with television raising the profiles of many star players, including Steve Davis, Cliff Thorburn, Terry Griffiths and Alex 'Hurricane' Higgins (left). The Northern Irishman won his first world championship in 1972 at the age of 22, then in 1982 he beat veteran Ray Reardon in the final to become world champion for the second and last time. Higgins got his nickname from his fast and furious style. By tradition snooker was played at a steady, studied pace, but he came in like a hurricane, strutting around the table and potting balls as fast as he could. While his opponent took a turn at the table, he spent the time smoking and drinking. At times volatile and unpredictable, Higgins once famously head-butted a referee during a match in 1986. But he created a new buzz around a staid sport and was always a favourite with snooker audiences and players alike. He died in July 2010.

BOOBY PRIZE
On 2 January, 1982, the rugby union international at Twickenham between England and Australia ground to a halt when a female streaker ran onto the pitch – much to the shock and delight of the crowd. The topless runner turned out to be a bookshop assistant from Hampshire named Erica Roe. Two policemen restrained her, evidently not without a good inspection of the offending articles. As they led her from the field, the policeman on the right managed to place his helmet decorously over Roe's left breast.

FROM PUB GAME TO PRIME TIME

Like snooker, darts became a regular and hugely popular fixture on the small screen during the Eighties. The most flamboyant character of the darts' decade was Eric Bristow, the 'Crafty Cockney', an East End lad from Hackney (above). He won the world championship no less than five times and was runner-up on three other occasions. Here he is with a trademark cigarette in his non-throwing hand, firing a dart during the 1984 World Championship. He went on to win, beating Dave Whitcombe 7-1 in the final. Other colourful players of the decade included Bobby George and Jocky Wilson, but Bristow's most consistent opponent was John Lowe, a joiner from Derbyshire who has the distinction of being the only player to win a world championship in three separate decades (in 1979, 1987 and 1993). In 1984 Lowe made dart history when he achieved the first nine-dart finish – the holy grail of dart players – in a televised tournament.

time at the relatively late age of 36. In the final he beat the hot favourite and world number one Steve Davis, then at the height of his considerable powers.

In tennis British players hardly featured at all, but a young West German named Boris Becker upset all predictions at Wimbledon. The favourites to win the men's singles title in 1985 were the defending champion John McEnroe and the number two seed, Ivan Lendl, but neither player made it to the final. With fearless athleticism in a sustained display of power and accuracy, Becker beat South African Kevin Curran three sets to one in the final to become, at just 17 years of age, the youngest player ever to win the championship.

Meanwhile, golf's biennial Ryder Cup had seen an unbroken procession of US wins since 1957. Whether facing Team Britain, Team Britain and Ireland, or Team Europe, the Americans had swept all before them. But in 1985 their 28-year run of success came to an end. At the Belfry Golf Club in Warwickshire, a European team captained by Tony Jacklin and packed with stars such as Ian Woosnam, Severiano Ballesteros, Sandy Lyle, Bernhard Langer and Nick Faldo finally and jubilantly brought the cup back to Europe.

Football dreams and nightmares

As for soccer, the early Eighties was a dismal time for Britain's national sides, but at least Scotland and England managed to reach the 1982 World Cup finals in Spain. Following England's repeated failures to qualify in the 1970s, this was success of a sort, but they failed to set the tournament alight. In the end Italy took the Jules Rimet trophy with a 3-1 win over Germany.

In marked contrast, the first half of the 1980s was a golden period for football clubs. Continuing the rich vein of form begun in the late Seventies, English teams maintained consistent success in the European Cup, winning a remarkable four out of the first five finals in the decade: Nottingham Forest in 1980, Liverpool in 1981, Aston Villa in 1982 and Liverpool again in 1984.

From hooligans to tragedies

The spectre of hooliganism had been present in British football throughout the previous decade, and in the 1980s it kept on rearing its ugly head. The *annus horribilis* was 1985. On 13 March, an FA Cup tie between Luton and Millwall witnessed one of the worst riots in the game's history, with thousands of so-called supporters fighting on the pitch.

On 11 May, 1985, a football tragedy struck in Bradford, when the Valley Parade stadium caught fire during a match against Lincoln City. The fire is thought to have started accidentally from a lighted cigarette or match falling on rubbish lying underneath an antiquated wooden stand. Around 11,000 spectators were present at the game and as the fire rapidly spread it claimed the lives of 56 people; more than 250 people were injured, many of them children. It was the worst disaster at a British football ground since 2 January, 1971, when the collapse of barriers on a stairway at Ibrox Stadium at the end of a Glasgow Rangers–Celtic game caused the deaths of 66 Rangers supporters.

TRIUMPH …
'Oh, it must be. It is. Peter Withe!' The words of commentator Brian Moore as he described the moment when Aston Villa scored the only goal in their victory over West German champions Bayern Munich in the European Cup final in Rotterdam on 27 May, 1982. Here (above), Tony Morley (on the left) and Villa captain Dennis Mortimer celebrate with the cup. It was Morley who set up the winning goal, making a run into the Bayern penalty area, turning the German full back inside out, then passing the ball across the face of the goal – the perfectly positioned Peter Withe then slotted it home.

... AND TRAGEDY

As the match against Lincoln City began on 11 May, 1985, Bradford City and their fans had every reason to cheer: they had just won promotion from the Third to the Second Division. But the atmosphere of celebration turned to panic and fear when the main stand caught fire. The spectators flocked onto the pitch to escape the flames (below), but 56 people lost their lives. The tragedy led to the Popplewell Report, which the following year made recommendations to improve fire safety in sports grounds. In 2010, the 25th anniversary of the fire was commemorated in Bradford city centre, where some 2,000 people gathered to sing 'You'll Never Walk Alone' before observing a minute's silence. In his address to the crowd John Sentamu, the archbishop of York, said that a community 'that forgets its memory becomes senile' and added, quoting Shakespeare, that 'praising what is lost makes remembrance dear'.

Neither the Ibrox nor Bradford City disasters had anything to do with crowd hooliganism, but at Heysel Stadium in Belgium the behaviour of a minority of fans led to yet another appalling tragedy. On 19 May, 1985, four-times European Cup winners Liverpool were playing in yet another final, this one against the Italian champions, Juventus. Before kick-off some Liverpool fans breached a fence intended to separate the rival supporters and attacked Juventus fans, who tried to escape. As more and more people retreated into one part of the stadium, a retaining wall collapsed crushing 39 people to death and injuring some 400 more.

It seems incredible today, but despite the disaster the authorities in Belgium decided to allow the game to be played: Juventus won, beating Liverpool by a single penalty. In the immediate aftermath UEFA, the governing body of European football, put the blame squarely on the Liverpool fans, some of whom were eventually charged with manslaughter in Belgium. On 31 May, under pressure from the Prime Minister, the Football Association banned English clubs from playing in Europe, pre-empting the same decision by UEFA two days later. Football clubs in Wales, Scotland and Northern Ireland were not affected by the ban, which cast English clubs into the wilderness until 1990 (1991 for Liverpool). A more considered investigation later came to the conclusion that a share of the blame also lay with the Belgian police and with the football authorities. Heysel

Stadium was judged to be in a poor state of repair – it would be demolished in 1994 – and Belgium was banned from hosting a European final for a decade.

One of the tactics introduced in the 1970s and 1980s to deal with hooliganism at football matches was to contain it, literally, by the introduction of enclosed cages in the spectator stands. This would backfire horrifically at the end of the decade in yet another mass tragedy – again involving Liverpool. At Hillsborough in Sheffield on 15 December, 1989, errors in crowd control led to far too many Liverpool fans being directed into one area of the ground as they flocked to watch their team take on Nottingham Forest in an FA Cup semi-final. As more and more fans piled in at the rear, the fence left fans at the front unable to escape. With the match live on television, millions watched helplessly as 93 Liverpool fans were crushed to death in the worst sporting disaster in Britain's history.

The 'hand of God'

The ban on clubs did not extend to the national team and in 1986 an England team managed by Bobby Robson played in the world cup finals in Mexico. In the quarter finals they faced Argentina, in an atmosphere charged with memories of the recent Falklands War. The game threw up two of the most famous goals in football, both of them scored by Argentina's star player. The first was a notorious handball that was obvious to everyone watching, but somehow went undetected by the referee. It became known as the 'hand of God' goal after Maradona's post-match comment that it owed something to the 'head of Maradona and to the hand of God'. But the second goal was a classic individual effort, with Maradona dribbling past six defenders to score. Lineker pulled a goal back, but it was Argentina who triumphed – and went on to win the cup.

After the match Maradona insisted that he had headed the ball, but years later in an interview with Gary Lineker he admitted he handled it. Maradona said that when he realised the referee had not seen the foul, he quickly celebrated with his teammates, leaving England's Shilton and Peter Reid to argue fruitlessly with the match official. Maradona's second goal settled the game. Lineker said of the Argentinian's amazing dribble and clinical finish that it was probably the only time in his career when he felt like applauding the opposition scoring a goal.

NEW TECHNOLOGY AND MEDIA

The 1980s were a time of rapid technological change, which dramatically affected the way of life in Britain. At the start of the decade people wrote letters by hand or typed them on manual typewriters, they listened to vinyl records and watched one of just four television channels. Phone calls were still made from coin-operated red telephone boxes. By the end of the decade computers had replaced typewriters, Compact Discs (CDs) had overtaken vinyl, Sky Television – using satellite technology – had doubled the number of TV channels available, and mobile phones were starting to make an impact.

Computers became central to life in the 1980s, evolving from the toys of a few dedicated enthusiastists to a mass-market product. IBM launched its first successful personal computer in August 1981, and three years later Apple unveiled the Macintosh with great fanfare. Many in Britain got their first taste of computing with the Sinclair ZX Spectrum, launched in April 1982 by the inventor Sir Clive Sinclair. Influential in its design and software, the elegant black ZX retailed for as little as £125, placing it within reach of the moderately well-off. Sinclair, who was a pioneer in pocket calculators, miniature TVs and digital watches, intended the ZX to be first and foremost a home computer. The model could run games such as Space Invaders and Pacman, already popular in arcades, and before long the ZX was selling 200,000 units a month. Sinclair produced upgraded versions of his computer; but eventually, in April 1986, he sold his business to the rival British company Amstrad, owned by Alan Sugar, for £5 million.

Sinclair's inventions could be hit or miss. His most high-profile failure was the C5 electronic trike, which looked like a low-slung white scooter. The theory was good: the battery-operated, affordable (it retailed at £399) vehicle was designed for short hops around town. But on the day of its launch on

A REVOLUTION TOO FAR
The inventor Sir Clive Sinclair launched his electric vehicle, the Sinclair C5, at Alexandra Palace in London on 10 January, 1985 (above). The BBC lined up Stirling Moss to give it a spin, and the former racing driver, though undoubtedly underwhelmed by the C5's top speed of 15mph, said that he thought it would be safe enough as long as people realised 'it isn't a car'. But the C5 was not one of Sinclair's successful inventions: far from revolutionising personal transport, it completely failed to take off with the public and proved to be a big financial loss-maker for its creator.

In the mid Eighties, some thought the mobile phone would go the same way. About the size and weight of a house-brick, it certainly would not fit into anyone's backpocket, but for some it instantly became a must-have piece of new technology – despite a price-tag in the region of £2,000. This businessman (left) shows off his new phone in conjunction with another essential item for the upwardly mobile in the Eighties: the Filofax

10 January, 1985, it was criticised for being too close to the ground and having inadequate visibility. The public were not convinced by it, and the C5 became something of a laughing stock. Only about 12,000 were sold, and Sinclair lost much of the money that the ZX had earned him.

CDs and mobiles challenge the status quo

The black vinyl disc had been the medium for recorded music for as long as anyone could remember. Records and their players had their problems – the vinyl surface was susceptible to scratches which would make the needle jump and fluff collected on the needle blurring the sound – but sound quality had improved immeasurably with the spread of stereos, which were now an essential component of any self-respecting music-loving household. But in the 1980s the vinyl record encountered a serious challenge when the Compact Disc, or CD, was launched. Two rival electronics firms, Philips and Sony, had joined forces to develop the latest in laser and optics technology, and came up with the small, shiny disc with rainbow tints that claimed – wrongly, as it turned out – to be scratch-proof.

The first pop album to be released in the CD format was *52nd Street* by Billy Joel in 1982. At first artists and the public – deterred by the high price of discs and CD players – were feeling their way. But in 1985 Dire Straits' album *Brothers in Arms* became the first to sell a million CDs. As prices for discs and

BRAVE NEW PC WORLD
The 1980s consolidated the growing role of computers in society. From being rare, outsized bits of kit in the previous decade, computers became more streamlined, user friendly and affordable – before long they would be essential items in the office, school and home, used by adults and children alike. Computer games quickly became popular: the young man on the right is playing Space Invaders, a popular arcade video game developed in Japan in the late Seventies and made available on PC. The idea was to shoot down as many invading aliens as you could.

players fell, the CD swept all before it, notwithstanding the nostalgic pinings of vinyl lovers, who grumbled about the smoother, allegedly less atmospheric, production values of the new format.

Telephones were fixed objects that lived at home – often in the hall – in the office or in telephone boxes. Car phones were known, but the idea of having a telephone that you could carry about and use anywhere was in the realm of fantasy. Then in mid-decade along came mobile phones. The first call on a mobile in the UK was made by the comedian Ernie Wise on 1 January, 1985, from St Katherine's Dock in London to Vodaphone's head office in Newbury in Berkshire. Wise had retired from performing following the death of his partner, Eric Morecambe, the previous year, but his enduring popularity and fame made him Vodaphone's choice to launch their revolutionary new technology.

PRINT REVOLUTION

Rupert Murdoch (above) realised that the new wave of computers was going to make creating and printing newspapers more efficient and cheaper. He was at the forefront of the print revolution, but it was Eddie Shah – seen below in the London editorial office of *Today* newspaper launched in 1986 – and not Murdoch who first tackled Britain's powerful print unions in order to bring new technology into newspaper production. Following Shah's successful action at his regional newspaper, Murdoch took on the far greater challenge of moving his newspaper premises from Fleet Street to Wapping and transforming production with new technology, with the consequent loss of jobs. Not surprisingly, he met fierce opposition among his workforce, but he simply sacked those who refused his terms. On 15 February, 1986, some 5,000 union members demonstrated outside Murdoch's Wapping plant and were met by hundreds of police with riot shields. Nearly 60 people were arrested and eight policemen were injured in the fracas, which both the police and union officials believed was caused by fringe elements. The bitterness of the strike rivalled that of the miners; it dragged on for a year, during which time more than 1,200 people were arrested and more than 400 police injured. One of those who tried to negotiate with Murdoch was Brenda Dean (above left), General Secretary of SOGAT (Society of Graphical and Allied Trades) and the first woman to lead a trade union in Britain. Twenty years after the dispute, Dean said: 'Given a little more time we could have negotiated but the die had been cast by Murdoch, his supporters and the Thatcher laws. The power was all on one side, and then it switched straight to the other. It was like a pendulum, and all the moderates like myself just got swept away.'

Making headlines

Advances in computers had an impact on many different industries, but none more so than the print media and publishing. At the end of 1983 Eddie Shah, owner of the *Stockport Messenger*, introduced new technology at his newspaper printworks in Warrington, thereby provoking a protest by the National Graphical Association (NGA) printers' union. Because of the new union legislation introduced by the Conservative government, Shah was able to take the union to court for taking 'secondary action'. It was the first salvo in a bitter struggle between newspaper owners and the print unions which would see a revolution in the way newspapers were produced and end with the demise of Fleet Street as the 'home of ink'.

In January 1986 a much larger and more protracted struggle erupted between the print unions and Rupert Murdoch, head of News International, the parent company of *The Times*, *News of the World* and the *Sun*. Australian-born Murdoch wanted to move his newspaper operation away from Fleet Street in central London to cheaper premises in Wapping in the East End. He also recognised the potential of new technology (he was to launch Sky Television in February 1989) and was determined to use the quicker and more efficient computer technology now available to produce his newspapers. Threatened with the loss of jobs, the print workers went on strike – and were promptly sacked.

News International ploughed ahead with the move to Wapping and managed to enlist the electricians' union, EETPU, to keep the newspapers rolling off the presses. In protest, the print unions organised pickets, marches and demonstrations outside the company's offices, but they came up against the new union legislation. After a year of bitter and at times violent protests, the print unions, threatened with court action and nearly bankrupt, had to accept defeat. It was a watershed in the history of the British press. Over the next few years the major newspapers all left Fleet Street to set up new operations in cheaper areas.

New technology had made it possible to topple the powerful print unions and it also gave rise to new opportunities for print entrepreneurs. In March 1986 Eddie Shah launched *Today* newspaper, a national tabloid intended to rival the *Daily Mail* and *Daily Express*. Then in October 1986 *The Independent* hit the newsstands, founded by three ex-Telegraph journalists, Andreas Whittam Smith, Stephen Glover and Matthew Symonds. The paper made much of its freedom from the influence of press barons as it trumpeted its editorial independence – its laconic advertising slogan was 'It is. Are You?' It was soon a favourite of the chattering classes and by the end of the decade it had a circulation of more than 400,000. *Today* proved less long-lived than the *Indie*, folding in 1995.

WEDDING BELLS
The second big royal wedding of the decade, between Prince Andrew and Sarah Ferguson, took place on 23 July, 1986. It was not quite the sumptuous fairy-tale that the wedding of Charles and Diana had been, but it was still an impressive affair. Andrew, who had seen active service in the Falklands War, wore dress navy uniform and Sarah looked radiant in her ivory satin dress, with the traditional long train extending 17ft (8ft shorter than Diana's). Archbishop of Canterbury Robert Runcie officiated at the ceremony in Westminster Abbey, Prince Edward was Best Man and Charles read a lesson. Foreign dignitaries who attended included America's First Lady, Nancy Reagan. Afterwards, the couple delighted the crowds waiting outside Buckingham Palace with a 'balcony kiss'. Then it was off to Claridges for a wedding banquet for 300 guests, followed by a honeymoon in the Azores.

HISTORIC TRIP

Throughout the Eighties the Queen was as busy as ever with royal engagements and often made one, sometimes two, state visits to foreign countries a year. Accompanied by Prince Philip she visited Norway in 1981, the USA in 1983 and Spain in 1988. Their trip to China in October 1986 made history by being the first visit to the country ever made by a British monarch. She and Prince Philip – seen here enjoying an exclusive stroll on part of the Great Wall – were received in Beijing by President Li Xiannian.

'There was this sense of a grand event …
something that would be stamped on everybody.
It was a day when, no matter how young you
were, you remembered where you were.

Gary Kemp of Spandau Ballet

CONCERT OF THE DECADE
Charles and Diana were just two
of more than 70,000 fans lucky
enough to have a ticket for
Wembley Stadium on 13 July,
1985 (above). Almost 100,000
were at the event in Philadephia.

Status Quo, Dire Straits, Queen
and U2 fronted by Bono (far
right) were among those playing
at Wembley. The Philadelphia
progamme (right) included a
reunited Crosy, Stills, Nash &
Young, Madonna, the Beach

Boys and Bob Dylan. Phil Collins
played at both events, crossing
the Atlantic on Concorde. Bob
Geldof performed early in the
day with the Boomtown Rats,
then concentrated on raising
money, telling viewers at home:

'You've got to get onto the
phone and take the money out
of your pocket. Don't go to the
pub tonight. Please stay in and
give us the money. There are
people dying now. So give me
the money!'

LIVE AID

After the success in December 1984 of the hit single 'Do They Know It's Christmas?', written by Bob Geldof and Midge Ure of Ultravox, the pair set about organising Live Aid to raise money for the victims of famine in Ethiopia. On 13 July, 1985, two simultaneous pop concerts were staged at Wembley in London and the JFK Stadium in Philadelphia, linked by the latest satellite technology, and watched live by an estimated 1.5 billion people. Geldof and Ure had persuaded some of the biggest names in rock and pop to perform for free, then between acts during the concert Geldof harangued the TV-viewing public to part with their money. The initial aim of raising more than £1 million through ticket sales was far exceeded, with charitable donations from around the world eventually topping an estimated £150 million.

LIVE AID CONCERT · JFK STADIUM

JULY 13, 1985 · PHILADELPHIA, PA.

LIVE AID COMPILATION
Following an opening tune from the band of the Coldstream Guards, it fell to Francis Rossi and veteran rockers Status Quo (left) to get the show on the road with 'Rockin' All Over the World'. Queen, with lead singer Freddie Mercury and guitarist Brian May (bottom left), gave one of the best performances of the day – in fact, a poll in 2005 voted their set the greatest live gig ever. The elegant Sade (right) was the only African-born performer on the bill. After dark, Tina Turner and Mick Jagger (far left) sang a duet of 'It's Only Rock'n'Roll' on the Philadelphia stage. Wembley closed with a moving rendition of 'Let it Be' by Paul McCartney followed by a finale featuring the Band Aid hit, 'Do They Know It's Christmas?' At the end of the concert, Pete Townshend of the Who and McCartney hoisted Bob Geldof on their shoulders (below).

'The sun was shining ... so were the people, and so were the bands.'

Bono of U2

THE **POWER** FADES

Mrs Thatcher and the Conservatives conducted their party conference of Autumn 1986 in a mood of infectious optimism. They were ahead of Labour in the opinion polls and speakers rallied the faithful under the slogan 'The Next Moves Forward', promising more privatisation, plans for new hospitals and reforms in education, criminal law and local government rates. The following spring, boosted by positive local election results and inflation running at just 4 per cent, Thatcher decided to go for an election that June, a year earlier than necessary.

MIRROR, MIRROR Margaret Thatcher in 1990, by which time her historic third term as Prime Minister, which started in a mood of optimism, had sunk into a pall of gloom, with troubles over the economy, Europe, the poll tax and cabinet resignations.

THATCHER'S HAT-TRICK

In the run-up to the general election on 11 June, 1987, Labour ran a slick campaign, quite unlike their shambolic election effort under Michael Foot. This time round the campaign was masterminded by Peter Mandelson and the highly telegenic Bryan Gould. The SDP-Liberal Alliance, with the two Davids, Owen and Steel, at the helm, huffed and puffed up their chances of winning outright victory, but their real hope lay in making a difference in a hung parliament. As Kinnock commented about the Alliance in the Labour manifesto: 'One of their leaders clearly favours an arrangement to sustain a Conservative government, the other hasn't the strength to stop him.'

The Tory campaign was not its most efficient, with party chairman Norman Tebbit unable to reproduce the silky smooth skills of Cecil Parkinson in 1983. Mrs Thatcher was nervous, even though victory seemed assured, particularly as the influential *Sun* was backing her to the hilt and running articles attacking Labour, such as 'Why I'm Backing Kinnock, by Stalin'.

In the end Thatcher need not have worried. The Conservatives won 376 seats to Labour's 229, giving Thatcher a hat-trick of election victories – a feat unseen since Lord Liverpool in the early 19th century. She increased her own share of the vote in her constituency of Finchley, seeing off, among others, Lord Buckethead of the Gremloid Party, a less vigorous opponent than Screaming Lord Sutch of the Monster Raving Loony Party had been in 1983. Thatcher celebrated into the night with her party workers and a relieved Tebbit. She warned them 'not to slack' since much was still to be done, particularly in the inner cities. Kinnock declared he would fight on and said that the Tories would create 'an even greater abyss of division than that which we witnessed previously'.

The Alliance, meanwhile, again failed to make the breakthrough it hoped for. Roy Jenkins lost his seat. When the dust had settled, David Steel proposed a full

1 MILLION COUNCIL HOMES HAVE BEEN SOLD TO THEIR TENANTS.

The Labour Party want to end tenants' automatic right to buy.

BRITAIN IS GREAT AGAIN. DON'T LET LABOUR WRECK IT.
VOTE CONSERVATIVE ☒

POLLS APART
The Conservative election campaign included this Saatchi & Saatchi-designed poster trumpeting the sale of council houses (above). Legislation brought in by the Tories in 1980 and 1985 gave council tenants new rights, allowing them, for example, to take lodgers or to swap homes with tenants in other areas. Above all, tenants could buy their flat or house after just two years residency, and by 1987 more than a million people had availed themselves of this opportunity.

The two Davids, Owen (on the left) and Steel, of the SDP-Liberal Alliance looking doubly glum after their disappointing election result. They parted ways after the 1987 general election. In August of that year the SDP MP Robert Maclellan, a Scottish barrister, became leader of the faction within the party that believed a full merger with the Liberals was the best way forward. A merger duly went ahead, but David Owen thought his Social Democrat principles were irreconcilable with those of the Liberal Party and decided instead to hang on as leader of a party of only three SDP MPs. But the days of his SDP were numbered. In May 1990, at a by-election in Bootle, the official SDP candidate polled less than half the votes for Screaming Lord Sutch and Owen finally realised it was time to wind the party up.

TRIUMPHANT TORIES
In a scene reminiscent of US-style elections, Margaret Thatcher's supporters celebrate on the night of her victory. The Tory campaign was helped by Nigel Lawson's vote-winning budget on 17 March, which cut the standard rate of income tax by 2 per cent. A couple of weeks after her victory, Mrs Thatcher went on a highly successful visit to Moscow, reminding Britons of her respected international standing. By contrast, Neil Kinnock and Denis Healey's trip to Washington at about the same time only served to demonstrate the US administration's disapproval of Labour's unilateralist nuclear policy. President Reagan mistook Healey for the British ambassador and gave the pair only 15 minutes of his time.

merger of the Liberals with the SDP and most of the influential voices in the latter agreed. So the Social and Liberal Democrat Party, later called the Liberal Democrats, was born. David Owen declined to join. David Steel stayed on as leader of the new party for a year, when he was replaced by the exuberant ex-Marine Paddy Ashdown.

STORMY WEATHER

Mrs Thatcher set about her third term with gusto. It was a period that would see her promote more MPs from the left of the party, such as Kenneth Clarke, Kenneth Baker, Douglas Hurd and John Major. But far from following her own free-market creed of trying to ensure that government interfered in people's lives as little as possible, this administration would launch a raft of reforms in education, the NHS and housing that saw a massive rise in direct government intervention.

THE GREAT STORM

On the night of 15-16 October, 1987, the worst storm since 1703 hit the southern counties of England. Roofs were blown off houses, balconies were torn off seaside apartments, scaffolding on numerous buildings came crashing down and countless trees were uprooted, many of them crushing cars where they fell. This residential street in Orpington, Kent (right), is typical of the scene that people woke up to – if they hadn't been kept awake by the storm – on the morning of 16 October. Many found they had no power, and no chance of going anywhere until someone cleared the debris from the roads. The south coast took the first brunt of the storm: two seamen were killed in Dover and a pier on the Isle of Wight was smashed to pieces. In Essex, a caravan park was utterly demolished. In some parts of the country the hurricane changed the landscape overnight – an estimated 15 million trees were lost. At Kew Gardens 700 rare and mature trees, many of them centuries old,

were uprooted. Brighton lost a magnificent avenue of elms, that had managed to survive Dutch elm disease. Another casualty was the *Hengist* (below), a Sealink passenger ferry that was blown aground at Folkestone. The storm caused damage estimated at £2 billion and took the lives of 18 people – the only reason the toll of casualties was not higher was because the worst of the winds hit in the middle of the night, when most people were asleep in their beds. Weather forecasters had predicted windy weather, but nothing like the hurricane-force 100mph-plus winds that actually arrived.

Such events are said to occur in Britain just once in a hundred years or more, but another storm of almost equal ferocity hit less than three years later. The Burns' Day Storm of 25-26 January, 1990, was actually more destructive than the Great storm because it struck during the day. It killed 47 people in Britain and caused damage estimated at more than £3 billion.

Fresh from electoral victory the Tories were in a mood to celebrate and went to their party conference in October 1987 with an almost hubristic sense of their invincibility. Within days, they and the nation were given a sharp reminder of the existence of unpredictable and destructive forces in both nature and finance.

On 16 October, a hurricane struck southern England, killing 18 people and injuring hundreds more. Three days later, Wall Street crashed. Black Monday, as it became known, saw share prices plummet across the world. In London, the FT 30-share index fell more than 180 points and £50 billion was wiped off the value of quoted shares at the Stock Exchange. The financial crash caused turmoil, but Britain slowly rode it out, with Nigel Lawson cutting interest rates in a bid to prevent recession.

'This is the nearest thing to a financial meltdown I've ever come across. I would not want to be around for another one like this.'

John Phelan, head of the New York Stock Exchange, commenting on Black Monday

Later on in that turbulent October, Mrs Thatcher, interviewed by *Woman's Own*, made her now-famous remark that 'there is no such thing as society'. The point she wanted to make was that 'society' is an abstraction – it is flesh-and-blood individuals, those who make up families and neighbours, that actually count. But many took the remark out of context to symbolise what they saw as her assault on communities and patronage of private greed. It became the catchphrase of anti-Thatcher commentators for years to come.

Gerbil and hospital trusts

In November 1987 the Tories began to reveal their key plans for their third administration. Nicholas Ridley unveiled his Housing Bill, which allowed council tenants to set up their own private trusts rather than remain under the control of local councils. The idea was to give local estates the power to be more self-reliant and improve their living conditions, but in practice very few trusts were set up.

Kenneth Baker disclosed his education reforms or 'Gerbil' – short for 'great education reform bill' – which included radical measures to let schools opt out of

NERVOUS TIMES
Traders at the London Stock Exchange had a nail-biting day watching a massive drop in share prices on 19 October, 1987 – aka 'Black Monday'. The press were quick to come up with alarmist headlines; the *Guardian* front-page read: 'Share rout in London and Wall St beats 1929 crash.' Two of the traders in the photograph are handling the new, must-have accessory in the City: the mobile phone.

the control of their local authorities. They also set up city technology colleges, ended academics' tenure at universities and implemented a national curriculum in schools. As Baker said, rather incoherently, of the latter: 'Somebody studying in Northumberland, if they had to move down to London, where were they? They'd already done dinosaurs twice and they'd do dinosaurs again there'. The bill, passed in 1988, would have a profound effect on the country's education.

There were proposed reforms of the NHS, the great money-guzzling behemoth which was always high on government agendas. Despite Thatcher's claims that the NHS was safe in Tory hands and that government spending on health had risen steadily during the Eighties, the public were unhappy with lengthening waiting lists and deferred operations. Health Secretary Kenneth Clarke proposed allowing hospitals to govern themselves as NHS Trusts, while general practitioners would have the option to become 'fundholders', which would give them direct control over their budgets to select suitable treatments for their patients. Against a background of increasing levels of private medical insurance, the plans were controversial, but over the years hospitals and an increasing number of doctors availed themselves of the chance to become self-financing.

The 'community charge' – a reform too far

The most radical and controversial government plan was the poll tax. For as long as anyone could remember, local government in Britain had been funded through rates, which was a charge on property rather than people and was based on property value. The government now proposed replacing rates with a 'community charge', whereby every adult, rather than every property, would be liable for a charge to be paid to their local council. Mrs Thatcher believed it was a fairer system, making everyone responsible for funding services in their local area. She also hoped that the 'community charge' would work against the higher-spending and therefore higher-taxing Labour-run councils.

But right from it's inception, the community charge was seen by the majority of the British public as intrinsically unfair. It was perceived as a poll tax by another name, and poll tax was the name that stuck. When the community charge bill was passed, in July 1988, it included some provision for the less well-off to claim a rebate on their contribution, but no amount of government persuasion could shift the general perception that the poll tax was iniquitous – that it was simply not right that an individual wealthy enough to live in a million-pound mansion should pay the same as someone in a low-paid job living in a shared house. For Thatcher it was a political time-bomb waiting to go off.

MUSIC TO MOVE TO

The early 1980s saw the New Romantics sweep the nation's youth away from the gloom of unemployment, riots, inflation and strikes into escapist fantasies. The distinctive Eighties music style that emerged from the movement and stayed throughout the decade was synthesiser or 'synth' pop and rock, in which drum-machines and electronic keyboards tapped out catchy hypnotic rhythms.

THE KING'S CROSS FIRE
At about 7.30pm on 18 November, 1987, King's Cross tube station became a terrifying inferno. The flames of the fire were probably whipped up by the blasts of wind created by trains arriving and departing at the underground platforms, and they soon engulfed the ticket hall, which was reduced to a burnt-out wreck (bottom right). Emergency services rushed to the scene (top) but they were unable to prevent the deaths of 31 people. The dead included one of the firefighters, Colin Townsley. King's Cross underground station processed about 100,000 travellers at rush hour, so there were initial fears that the death toll might be much higher.

The investigation into the cause of the fire concluded it had probably been started by a lighted match, unwittingly dropped through an old wooden escalator, igniting bits of rubbish and grease on machinery below. Smoking had been prohibited on tube trains since 1984, and the ban was extended to platforms and other parts of London Underground stations after a fire at Oxford Circus in February 1985. Nevertheless, some smokers still reached for their matches and cigarettes as they left the stations. An official enquiry resulted in legislation in 1989 that required London Underground to replace wooden escalators with metal ones, install automatic sprinklers and implement fire training for staff.

COOL MOVES

Breakdancing required rhythm and athleticism in equal measure. It originated in New York's Bronx in the 1970s and was popularised by films such as *Flashdance*, released in 1983 – the same year that this young man was spotted on a UK street.

The Police – Sting (aka Gordon Sumner), Andy Summers and Stewart Copeland – were at the height of their fame early in the decade. They are seen above performing in 1983, the year they released their last album, *Synchronicity*. They disbanded to follow solo careers the following year.

Yet at the same time, more traditional mainstream music carried on unaffected, just as it had during the punk era in the Seventies. Indie groups such as the Smiths and Stone Roses had cult followings, while rock bands such as U2, Simple Minds and Dire Straits, as well as solo artists such as David Bowie, Phil Collins, Michael Jackson and Madonna, sold albums in the millions. For the teenie boppers there were the likes of Jason Donovan, Kylie Minogue and Bros, a trio of likely lads from Peckham in London, featuring twins Luke and Matt Goss.

The 'Madchester' scene

Outside London, the principal musical powerhouse was Manchester; by the end of the decade the city had become one of the hippest centres of music and youth culture in Europe. Manchester was put on the music map in the early Eighties by

THE NEW CULTURE SCENE

One of the few New Romantic bands to achieve chart success in both the UK and the US was Culture Club, featuring (from left to right) singer Boy George, drummer Jon Moss, Roy Hay on guitar and keyboards and Mikey Craig on bass. Boy George cultivated a deliberately androgynous look that harked back to the days of David Bowie's Ziggy Stardust, but without the cosmic pretensions. His impish persona was a large part of Culture Club's appeal, while his laid-back vocals perfectly suited the band's mixture of pop, reggae and soul. In 1982 the band had a smash hit with 'Do You Really Want to Hurt Me', which topped the UK charts and reached No 2 in the USA. The following year 'Karma Chameleon' went one better, reaching No 1 in both countries.

the independent record label Factory Records, which had started life as a club founded by Alan Erasmus and Tony Wilson in 1978. There was also the Haçienda nightclub, located in a converted Victorian textile factory and funded by Factory Records and one of the label's early bands, New Order. Made up of Bernard Sumner on vocals and various instruments, Gillian Gilbert on keyboards, Stephen Morris on drums and Peter Hook on bass, New Order had risen from the ashes of Joy Division, who had been blown apart in 1980 by the tragic suicide of lead-singer and songwriter Ian Curtis. The new band combined synthesiser pop with an indie-rock edginess and their influence far exceeded their chart success. New Order scored top-ten hits with 'Blue Monday' in 1983 and 'True Faith' in 1987, but had to wait until 1990 to top the UK singles chart with 'World in Motion', sung in association with the England world cup football squad – and featuring Liverpool forward John Barnes doing a nifty mid-song bit of rapping.

Perhaps most influential of all in cementing Manchester's musical reputation were the Smiths, a band formed in 1982 that managed to retain its cult appeal while becoming hugely popular. Fronted by the enigmatic Morrissey on vocals and featuring Johnny Marr on guitar, the Smiths wove tales of alienation, love and

MADCHESTER MEN
Morrissey and Johnny Marr (left), the song-writing partnership of the Smiths, on stage at Manchester Free Trade Hall in March 1984. The other band members were Andy Rourke (bass) and Mike Joyce (drums). The Smiths released their first album through the independent label Rough Trade Records in 1984 and achieved instant success on the album chart – in fact their first four albums, *The Smiths*, *Meat is Murder*, *The Queen is Dead* and *Strangeways, Here We Come* charted respectively at 2, 1, 2 and 2. This was not mirrored on the singles chart, perhaps because some of their subject matter – such as vegetarianism, corporal punishment and most controversially the Moors murders – was far from the usual pop fare. But their work was not insensitive and was leavened with lyrical touches and a dry sense of humour.

The Stone Roses formed in Manchester in 1984. They were fronted by vocalist Ian Brown, seen here (above) performing in 1987. Their big breakthrough came in 1989 with their debut album, *The Stone Roses*, which in 2004 was hailed by an *Observer* newspaper poll as the best UK album of all time, knocking the Beatles' *Revolver* into second place.

loneliness that struck a chord across many musical tastes. They were a breath of fresh air with a unique sound that stood out from the all-pervading synth pop. By the time the Smiths broke up, in 1987, Manchester was established as a major hub of music, with a distinctive independent rock and dance music scene. Bands such as the Stone Roses, Inspiral Carpets and the Happy Mondays released influential singles, and the Haçienda was throbbing to Acid House music. In the following year the music press recognised 'Madchester' as the vibrant music scene it was, and both the Roses and Mondays appeared on *Top of the Pops*, bringing their brand of indie music to a mass audience.

Another 'summer of love'

In 1988 a new soundtrack exploded onto the music scene that would define the late Eighties: Acid House. In a period loosely called the 'summer of love' (or the 'second summer of love' in deference to the one in 1967), nightclubs and disused warehouses all over the country throbbed to the techno beat of House music, while thousands of happy young people danced into a trance-like state. At first, even the *Sun* saw little to criticise in the new youth craze – the music might be repetitive, but the teenagers seemed to like it and were obviously having fun, as epitomised by the yellow Smiley logo on their T-shirts. But gradually it dawned on the adult world that the dervish-like energy was not purely the result of youthful exuberance or the ice-pops and Lucozade the dancers drank to cool down

Acid House originated in Chicago, taking its name not from LSD, the Sixties drug also known as acid, but more probably from a pop single called 'Acid Trax' released by a band named Phuture. Acid House bands, such as KLF and 808 State, produced music that thrummed with drum machines and synthesisers, and their long, mesmerising tracks were the perfect soundtrack for trance-like dancing. The music reached the club scene in Ibiza in the mid Eighties, where it was picked up by young Britons on holiday. By 1987 a few clubs in London, Sheffield and Manchester – the Shoom run by Danny Rampling, the Haçienda – were introducing the new synth sound. The following year Acid House exploded.

Enter Ecstasy

The match that lit the Acid House fuse was a drug called Ecstasy, which was introduced from Amsterdam. Ecstasy, or 'E', has the effect of making users euphoric, light-headed, uninhibited and carefree: it was the perfect match for the music. Not everyone who was into Acid House music was also into Ecstasy, but generally speaking, from here on, the two went hand in hand.

The new club trend spawned a new fashion look. Clubbers, infused with endless energy in steaming hot clubs, found baggy clothes more suitable than tight jeans. Loose trousers, dungarees, trainers, bandanas and T-shirts became the order of the day as people dressed down rather than up for the night. This House uniform in turn helped to promote a sense of great intimacy and comradeship. Music journalist John McCready described how, before the advent of Acid House, clubs were '… full of apprentices in pressed white shirts on the pull. Girls were huddled in groups like disorientated wildebeest.' Out went the gauche chat-up lines, sharp suits and little black numbers to be replaced by a heaving, unisex mass of baggy-clothed youth dancing hour after hour, in worlds of their own.

From clubs to fields

It was not long before Acid House shifted from the clubs to improvised venues as private parties grew into mass 'raves'. In August 1988 a huge rave took place at Wembley Studios and ITN cameras were allowed in. Parents now became more concerned about what their children were getting up to. On 17 August the *Sun* reported on Acid House at the Heaven club (then owned by Richard Branson) and alarmed its readers with reports of 'drug-crazed junkies'.

Then came the first widely reported tragedy. Janet Mayes, a young clubber, died on 28 October, 1988, after taking two Ecstasy tablets. From now on the tabloids fuelled widespread alarm about Acid House and the police, who had taken little notice of raves, began to break them up. Yet the craze continued unabated, perhaps attracting even more young people after all the publicity.

By November 1988 raves were becoming more organised. Small groups of promoters – two of the first were Genesis and Sunrise – staged events in empty warehouses, turning them into instant giant clubs with sound systems and lights. From 1989, raves moved outdoors into fields and airfields, sometimes attracting thousands of young people. The trick for the organisers was to keep the event venue secret – to put the police off the scent – until the very last moment.

HOUSE MEMBERS
Dancers silhouetted against a multi-coloured kaleidoscopic light-show in a typical club scene at the end of the 1980s. 'Hot night' at the Haçienda in Manchester featured a swimming pool where dancers could cool off with a dip. After closing time at the Spectrum at Heaven or the Trip at the Astoria, clubbers would spill out to revel in central London fountains, initially to the bemusement of police who found no evidence of alcohol abuse.

Motorway service stations became meeting points. Many ravers simply followed the car in front in the hope of being led to the party. Many sites lay around London's M25, nicknamed Orbital raves. Sleepy home counties' towns and villages would suddenly see the unannounced arrival of thousands of youngsters accompanied by sound systems as loud as aircraft engines.

Acid House, raves and Ecstasy survived into the 1990s. But the government, the press and public opinion were now against them, and as the original promoters lost their initial enthusiasm the movement gradually fizzled out. But for a brief period Acid House created a 'summer of love' to rival that of 1967, transporting many of the nation's youth far from the realities of Thatcher's Britain.

MUSIC AND FASHION

In most decades, music and fashion go hand in hand, but rarely have they been so linked as in the New Romantic movement of the early 1980s. Bands such as Adam and the Ants, Duran Duran, Culture Club, Spandau Ballet and their fans donned make-up, quiffs and flouncy shirts and made a virtue of flamboyance. In complete contrast, the decade ended with the repetitive thumping beat and low grunge couture of Acid House. In between, indie and alternative voices came to the fore: the Eurythmics, Simply Red, the Smiths and stadium rockers Simple Minds and U2. Solo singers Rick Astley and Kylie Minogue scored huge hits thanks to the songwriting and producing talents of Stock, Aitken and Waterman, whose synthesiser-pop sound was ubiquitous in the charts.

NEW ROMANTICS, NEW MEN Stuart Leslie Goddard, better known as Adam Ant (right), was at the vanguard of the New Romantic pop bands, setting new fashion trends. Adam and the Ants scored their greatest success in 1981 with two chart-topping singles 'Stand and Deliver' and 'Prince Charming'.

Andrew Ridgely (below right) and George Michael (left) were two school friends who shot to global stardom as Wham!. Image-conscious and media-savvy, they presented themselves as sunny, fun-loving guys. Their breakthrough on *Top of the Pops* came with 'Young Guns (Go for It!)' in 1982, then the hits came thick and fast: 'Wake Me Up Before You Go-Go', 'Freedom', 'Last Christmas'. By the time they split in 1986, they had sold more than 25 million albums.

ALL IN THE LOOK

The crucible of the New Romantics was London's Blitz Club, which for a while employed Boy George (pre-Culture Club fame) as a cloakroom attendant. The Blitz kids, as they were known – some of them shown here dancing in 1981 (right) – displayed quiffs, satins, scarves, frilly shirts, jumpsuits and generous amounts of mascara in one great gender-bending mélange. Other Eighties fashions included high-hair styles – as on these young women (above) seen on Chelsea's Kings Road in 1981 – which owed something to the hair of both Punk and Glam rock. Trousers range from drainpipes to baggy pleats, while fitted jackets, frilly collars and simple tops were all considered chic. Unlike Punk rockers, New Romantics tried to follow a style while not looking like anyone else.

FAMOUS EIGHTIES FACES
Adored by Princess Diana and admired by Andy Warhol, Duran Duran were one of the biggest bands of the 1980s, reaching a peak of fame between 1983 and 1985. Quite apart from the music, they recognised the importance of image and brought in fashion designers to develop their look. They were also one of the first to use professional directors for their videos. Promotional shots like this one (right) of lead singer Simon Le Bon (on the left) and bassist John Taylor quickly turned them into teenage heartthrobs. They registered several massive hits in the decade, including 'Rio', 'Is There Something I Should Know?' and 'The Reflex', and were one of the few British bands to make it big in the USA. They also proved long-lived: at the last count they had sold more than 100 million albums and were still touring.

Distinctive Scottish singer Annie Lennox, seen here (left) in 80s-style pearly queen leather, teamed up with English musician Dave Stewart in the Eurythmics, a pop band with an alternative edge. The combination of bass-driven synthesiser music with Lennox's powerful vocals gave them a string of hits, including 'Sweet Dreams (Are Made of This)' and 'Who's That Girl?'. They enjoyed pushing the boundaries, often collaborating with other musicians from Stevie Wonder to Elvis Costello.

With fashionable ripped jeans and gelled hair, Peckham twins Matt and Luke Goss – Luke is playing the keyboard (top right) – made Bros the boy band of the late Eighties. Their mainly female fans were known as Brosettes.

Siobhan Fahey, Keren Woodward and Sara Dallin blazed a trail for all-girl bands as Bananarama (bottom right). Hits included 'Shy Boy' 'Robert De Niro's Waiting', 'Venus' and 'Love in the First Degree'. The big hair and baggy chic was a typical look in the decade.

TENSIONS AT HOME AND ABROAD

In January 1985 the bespectacled, thoughtful Jacques Delors had become the eighth President of the European Commission. Delors was a French economist and socialist who fervently believed in the European project and was committed to bringing about economic and monetary union (EMU). In a speech in July 1988 he went further, referring to the possibility of a European government being formed within a few years. Thatcher respected Delors as a politician, but liked neither his socialist credentials nor his aims for an integrated Europe and a week after his speech publicly rebuked him in an interview on Radio 2's Jimmy Young Show.

On 8 September, 1988, in what became a significant moment in British politics, Delors addressed the TUC conference in Bournemouth. He charmed the delegates with his vision of a Europe open to collective bargaining and legislation to safeguard workers' rights, and was given a standing ovation and a chorus of 'Frère Jacques'. The TUC and a large section of the Labour Party had always been hostile to the European project, but Delors had changed their perception almost overnight. Perhaps Brussels was a more sympathetic place than a Tory-run Britain?

The Bruges speech

Conversely, throughout her premiership Thatcher had supported much of the European project – albeit with strong reservations – especially given Labour's hostility towards it. These roles were now reversing. And if there was one moment that hastened the Conservatives' change of heart, it was the speech Mrs Thatcher delivered in Bruges in September 1988.

She began positively, praising the Belgian medics who saved the lives of so many Britons after the Zeebrugge ferry disaster on 6 March, 1987. Most of the speech had a pro-European flavour and she even cracked a joke: 'If you believe some of the things said and written about my views on Europe, it must seem rather like inviting Genghis Khan to speak on the virtues of peaceful coexistence!' Then she laid her cards on the table: 'We have not successfully rolled back the frontiers of the state in Britain, only to see them reimposed at a European level, with a European super-state exercising a new dominance from Brussels.' Her words were a blatant rejection of Delors and EU ambitions.

The speech caused a storm of controversy. It delighted latent Eurosceptics of all political shades back in Britain but dismayed the pro-Europeans. Sir Geoffrey Howe, who had worked so hard to improve Britain's relations with Europe, likened the episode to 'being married to a clergyman who had suddenly proclaimed his disbelief in God'. From now on, Europe would be the Tories' Achilles heel, the issue which the opposition could attack, knowing that each jab would exacerbate divisions within the party.

> **'Working more closely together does not require power to be centralised in Brussels ...'**
> Margaret Thatcher, speaking in Bruges, September 1988

The hostage crisis

The Middle East was as dangerous and volatile in the second half of the Eighties as it was in the first. The Iran–Iraq war ended only in August 1988. Civil war was raging in Lebanon and Beirut, its devastated capital, was full of conflicting militias, backed by bigger powers in the region. Westerners in the city risked losing their lives – or being kidnapped.

In April 1986 the British journalist John McCarthy and Irish teacher Brian Keenan were separately kidnapped by members of the militant Islamic Jihad. Early in the following year Terry Waite, special envoy of the archbishop of Canterbury, Robert Runcie, arrived in Beirut to try to secure their release but he, too, was taken prisoner on 20 January. Diplomatic overtures to end the hostage saga continued through the rest of the decade. Runcie, for example, appealed to Iran to use its influence. The campaign that was most effective at keeping the crisis in the public eye was that mounted by Jill Morrell, McCarthy's girlfriend. Her unflagging efforts gained widespread admiration.

Death in Lockerbie

On 21 December, 1988, PanAm flight 103 en route from London to New York exploded over the town of Lockerbie in Scotland. All 259 passengers and crew on board the jumbo jet were killed, as well as 11 people in Lockerbie itself. The plane victims came from 21 countries, but 190 of them – the vast majority – were US citizens; 32 of the passengers and crew were British. In the following years, a massive investigation was conducted in an attempt to track down those responsible for the atrocity, a trail that led eventually to Libya.

KEEPING VIGIL
The campaign to free the Middle East hostage John McCarthy was driven by his girlfriend Jill Morrell (above, centre). Morrell founded the Friends of John McCarthy to keep his name in the public eye and put pressure on the government to do everything it could to secure his release. The group organised candlelit vigils and produced posters, badges and adverts to highlight McCarthy's plight.

John McCarthy was released by his captors – he saw 'the bright glaring light', to use Morrell's words – in August 1991, five years after his disappearance. Although the nation hoped for a happy romantic ending, McCarthy and Morrell split up in 1995 – amicably and after they had written the best-selling *Some Other Rainbow*. As McCarthy said later: 'Adjusting to the real world was much more difficult than I'd imagined. I had assumed you would just come home.'

SURVIVING DAY TO DAY

Brian Keenan (right) was eventually freed in August 1990. He returned to his home in Northern Ireland and wrote *An Evil Cradling,* an account of the years that he was held hostage in Lebanon, which was published in 1993. His words simply yet vividly recount the horror of what he went through. 'For several months, I was held in isolation and complete darkness in a cockroach and rat-infested cell.' After his capture, all his clothes and personal belongings were taken from him: 'I was made to wear a blindfold and a pair of shorts ... For the first two years I was given no books or papers or allowed any access to radio or TV. Nor was I told who was holding me or why.'

Church of England envoy Terry Waite, seen below in a photograph taken in Libya in 1986, was involved in several successful negotiations to free hostages before his ill-fated trip to Beirut in January 1987. When he went to meet with the hostages' captors, he was taken prisoner himself and held in solitary confinement for the first four years. The first word his family heard of him was from Brian Keenan, who visited them after his release. Terry Waite was eventually freed in November 1991.

RAINING DEATH IN LOCKERBIE
Wreckage from PanAm 103, the 747 blown out of the sky by a terrorist bomb, lies strewn in and around the Scottish town of Lockerbie (left). The falling debris caused considerable damage on the ground, destroying houses and killing 11 people in Lockerbie itself. All 259 passengers and crew on board the plane.

During the next three years, police from the local Dumfries and Galloway force, along with US FBI agents, investigated the bombing. In 1991 they accused two Libyans, Abdelbaset Ali al-Megrahi and Lamin Khalifah Fhimah, of carrying out the atrocity and called on Libya's leader, Colonel Gaddafi, to hand the men over for trial. Gaddafi first offered to try the men in Libya, but not elsewhere. In 1992 the UN ordered Libya to hand over the men; when this demand met with refusal, sanctions were imposed on the country. By 1998, feeling the pressure of the sanctions, Gaddafi agreed in principle to allow the two men to be tried under Scottish law, but in a neutral country. The following year, following an intercession by Nelson Mandela, Colonel Gaddafi handed over the two men to stand trial in the Netherlands. In 2001 the court acquitted Lamin Khalifah Fhimah but found Abdelbaset Ali al-Megrahi guilty. He was sentenced to 27 years in prison, to be served in Scotland.

Al-Megrahi always claimed he was innocent and was appealing against the conviction when he was diagnosed with terminal prostate cancer in 2009. He was released on compassionate grounds in August that year and returned to Libya. The decision to free him caused huge controversy and much anger – especially among Americans, of whom 190 died in the bombing.

The gulf between east and west

Less than two months after the Lockerbie bombing, on St Valentine's Day 1989, the Iranian leader Ayatollah Khomeini issued a fatwa in which he condemned to death the British novelist Salman Rushdie. Khomeini accused Rushdie of blaspheming the Prophet Muhammad in his book *The Satanic Verses*, a charge that Rushdie denied.

Demonstrations against Rushdie's book had already taken place in various Muslim countries and also in Britain – copies were publicly burnt in Bradford. The British government protested, but there was little that could be done other than give Rushdie police protection.. He was forced to live in hiding for almost a decade. Only in 1998, when the president of Iran, Muhammad Khatami, declared that his country would not support the fatwa (which is technically irrevocable), did Rushdie come out of hiding.

Death on the Rock

The Middle East was not the only political hot spot – the troubles in Northern Ireland had not gone away, either. The Hillsborough Agreement, signed in 1985, had given a measure of cautious hope to those inside and outside the province who longed for a solution. But sectarian violence, and reaction by the security forces, continued to damage morale and sabotage the efforts of moderates.

One particularly controversial incident occurred on Gibraltar on 6 March, 1988, when the SAS shot dead three unarmed IRA members. The IRA admitted that the two men and one woman comprised an active service unit, and bomb materials were afterwards found in one of their cars. But the fact that they were unarmed and only acting suspiciously, rather than caught in an illegal act, caused Foreign Secretary Sir Geoffrey Howe and the government great embarrassment.

The Gibraltar episode also had a bloody coda. On 16 March a huge crowd were at Milltown Cemetery in Belfast attending the funerals of the three IRA dead when a loyalist gunman, Michael Stone, began shooting and throwing grenades. He killed three of the mourners and wounded more than 50. Although he escaped his pursuers, he was later arrested, tried and sentenced to a minimum of 30 years imprisonment. Three days later, during the funeral of one of Stone's victims, two British corporals accidentally drove near the cortege: they were abducted, stripped, beaten and shot. Some of the harrowing scenes leading to their deaths were caught on camera and shocked the nation.

TOWARDS THE END GAME

The final year of the decade was a momentous one for Europe, with the fall of the Berlin Wall in November and revolts against communist rule in Poland, Czechoslovakia, Hungary and elsewhere. Compared with such events, British politics seemed relatively serene, but in fact Mrs Thatcher was having her most difficult year as leader so far.

The year began with the hangover from the 'salmonella affair', which blew up in the last weeks of 1988. Edwina Currie, the colourful junior health minister,

KEEPING A STRAIGHT FACE
One of the more colourful figures in Mrs
Thatcher's second government was Jeffrey
Archer, a flamboyant millionaire novelist
who was appointed Deputy Chairman of the
Conservative Party in 1985. His tenure
lasted only a year: in the autumn of 1986
the *Daily Star* alleged that Archer had been
involved with a prostitute named Monica
Coughlan. He resigned his post and the
following year sued the *Star* for libel. Archer
won the case, but retribution was to come.
In 2000, two of his former associates
accused him of perjury in the 1987 trial.
This time Archer lost his case and was
sentenced to four years for perjury and
perverting the course of justice.

For all his misdemeanours and
indiscretions, Archer was continually
involved in charity work. Here he is shown
in his Thames-side apartment in 1988
sporting a red nose as part of Comic Relief,
a charity founded in 1985 that harnessed
the nation's top comedians and celebrities
in a fund-raising telethon broadcast on the
BBC. Since Red Nose Day was launched in
1988 millions of plastic red noses have
been sold in aid of the charity and worn by
people – and cars – all over the country.

pronounced on television that 'Most of the egg production in this country, sadly,
is now infected with salmonella'. Newspaper headline writers had a field day
with 'egg' puns, but her words infuriated egg producers, as well as colleagues at
the Ministry of Agriculture. Thatcher initially backed Currie, but in the end,
threatened by legal action from the farming industry, Currie resigned.

Strained relations

The Tories, especially the hard-core monetarists, had made lowering inflation a
badge of pride. But during the government's third term the spending boom of the
mid-Eighties, coupled with deregulation of the City, overheated the economy and
inflation began to rise. After the Stock Exchange crash in 1987, Nigel Lawson's
decision to cut interest rates to stave off recession made the economy grow faster
than was good for it. Then in March 1988 he cut taxes, reducing the top rate from
60 to 40 per cent. With more money in their pockets, consumers bought more and
inflation went up. Now, he was having to raise interest rates to tackle inflation,
which by the decade's end it was close to 10 per cent.

The rise in inflation put a strain on the already uneasy relationship between
Thatcher and Lawson. Another crucial difference between them was Lawson's
intention of joining the Exchange Rate Mechanism (ERM), a move supported by
Sir Geoffrey Howe and most of the cabinet but rejected by Thatcher who feared
it would lead to a single European currency. As she turned increasingly to her
personal economic adviser, Sir Alan Walters, it became clear that she was losing
faith in Lawson, whose popularity and standing made him impossible to sack.

Isolated from Lawson at the Treasury and Howe at the Foreign Office,
Thatcher had few dyed-in-the-wool supporters in cabinet and turned increasingly
to her own advisers. Her domineering style had been criticised by Michael
Heseltine after the Westland affair. Now it was talked about as a major failing.
As she approached her tenth anniversary in May 1989, she could hardly ignore
the new economic and political difficulties besetting her government.

Poll tax protests

The poll tax was introduced in Scotland on 1 April, 1989 – a year before its
implementation in England and Wales. As the Scots saw it, they were being used
as guinea pigs for the English, and vented their anger. In Edinburgh 25,000 people
marched against the tax, and the Scottish TUC put on a high-profile pop concert
in the Usher Hall as part of the 'Rock Against the Poll Tax' protest. The
demonstrations inaugurated a campaign of mass non-payment of the tax, which
the government was quite unable to counter. And the situation would get far
worse the following year.

Thatcher challenged

In June, just before a European summit in Madrid, Howe and Lawson implied
to the Prime Minister that they would resign over her opposition to Britain joining
the ERM. She backed down in the face of their joint threat, but got her revenge in
July when she removed Howe from the Foreign Office and transferred him
unceremoniously to the post of Leader of the House of Commons. John Major,
a relative unknown at the time, replaced him. Howe was clearly upset by this
demotion, and although Thatcher brazened out the switch of jobs, she had greater
difficulty riding out Lawson's resignation on 26 October. In addition to the issue

of the ERM, Lawson felt undermined. To fill the breach at the Treasury, she replaced him with Major and made Douglas Hurd Foreign Secretary. Although she claimed, truthfully, that Major and Hurd were magnificently suited to jobs they had always aspired to, there was a sense of wheels loosening on the Tory juggernaut and the driver losing her grip. It was her most damaging nine months in power. There were whisperings among Tories about a change of leader, but they remained *sotto voce* until November 1989, when Sir Anthony Meyer, a backbench MP, stepped forward to challenge Mrs Thatcher for the leadership. It was the first such contest she had faced during her premiership

Meyer, an avid pro-European, had long been disillusioned by Thatcher's anti-Europe rhetoric. He knew he would be obliterated, but saw himself as a stalking horse for someone with greater authority to mount a more credible bid. The press were merciless, labelling Mayer 'Sir Nobody' and 'a stalking donkey'. In the vote on 5 December, he polled only 33 to Thatcher's 314. But 27 MPs had either spoiled their ballot papers or not cast a vote, which meant that Thatcher had lost the support of 60 MPs – a sixth of the parliamentary party.

Thatcher put the best spin possible on the result, appearing outside No. 10 to tell the press: 'I would like to say how very pleased I am … to have had the overwhelming support of my colleagues in the House and the people from the party in the country.' Party chairman Kenneth Baker rowed in, too, with soothing words: 'What the Conservative Party has decided today is that they want to be led into the 1990s and the next election by Margaret Thatcher.'

But the reality was very different. As the Eighties drew to a close, with European communist governments falling like skittles, so the tremors leading to Mrs Thatcher's eventual downfall grew stronger. Meyer had irrevocably damaged the Prime Minister's aura of invincibility. As he later said: 'It made the unthinkable thinkable'. Within a year, the unthinkable had happened.

AND ONE MORE THING …
Mrs Thatcher on the doorstep at Downing Street on 4 May, 1989, the tenth anniversary of becoming Prime Minister.

INDEX

PICTURE ACKNOWLEDGEMENTS

Abbreviations: t = top; m = middle; b = bottom; r = right; c = centre; l = left
All images in this book are courtesy of Getty Images, including the following which have additional attributions:

Front cover: David Montgomery
Back cover, 124, 154t, 159: Georges DeKeerle
2, 110t: Redferns/Virginia Turbett
4, 34, 69r, 103, 120: SSPL
6-7: Dave Hogan
8-9, 138: Leon Morris
10-11, 12-13, 77, 79: Steve Eason
17, 68, 74, 75, 106, 113, 126b, 127b, 133: Popperfoto
19l, 92, 100b, 107, 121: Time & Life Pictures
22, 24, 25r, 70, 112, 115: Bob Thomas Sports Photography

23t: IOC Olympic Museum
31, 105, 111tr, 111bl, 145: Redferns/ David Corio
39, 45, 54, 62, 71, 87, 119b, 128, 132, 137t, 152, 153b: John Downing
41, 43, 50, 57, 154b: Agence France Presse
52, 122, 123: Tim Graham Photo Library
63t, 66t, 67, 84t, 134: Tom Stoddart
66b: The Conservative Party Archive
88: Kaveh Kazemi
100t, 153t: Gemma Levine

104: Redferns/Erica Echenberg:
111br, 160: Terry O'Neill
114b: Chris Smith
119t: David Levenson
125l: Blank Archives
139t: Redferns/Rob Verhorst
141r: Redferns/Suzie Gibbons
141l: Redferns/Martin O'Neill
143: Redferns/Phil Dent
144: Redferns/Peter Still
146: Janette Beckman
147: Homer Sykes
149b: Redferns/Ebet Roberts

LOOKING BACK AT BRITAIN
THATCHER'S BRITAIN – 1980s
Published in 2010 in the United Kingdom by
Vivat Direct Limited (t/a Reader's Digest) in association
with Getty Images and Endeavour London Limited

Vivat Direct Limited
(t/a Reader's Digest)
157 Edgware Road
London W2 2HR

Endeavour London Limited
21–31 Woodfield Road
London W9 2BA
info@endeavourlondon.com

Copyright © 2010 Vivat Direct Limited

Colour origination by Chroma Graphics Ltd, Singapore
Printed and bound in Europe by Arvato Iberia, Portugal

For Endeavour
Publisher: Charles Merullo
Designer: Tea Aganovic
Picture editors: Jennifer Jeffrey, Franziska Payer Crockett
Production: Mary Osborne

For Vivat Direct
Editorial director: Julian Browne
Art director: Anne-Marie Bulat
Project editor: Christine Noble
Art editor: Conorde Clarke
Indexer: Marie Lorimer
Proofreader: Ron Pankhurst
Pre-press technical manager: Dean Russell
Product production manager: Claudette Bramble
Production controller: Sandra Fuller

Written by
James Harpur

We are committed both to the quality of our products
and the service we provide to our customers.
We value your comments, so please do contact us on
08705 113366 or via our website at
www.readersdigest.co.uk

If you have any comments or suggestions about
the content of our books, email us at
gbeditorial@readersdigest.co.uk

CONCEPT CODE: UK 0154/L/S
BOOK CODE: 638-014 UP0000-1
ISBN: 978 0 276 44402 9
ORACLE CODE: 356900014H.00.24